D1447084

BRIDGETON
NEW JERSEY

CITY ON THE COHANSEY

SHARRON MORITA

Charleston London

THE
History
PRESS

Published by The History Press
Charleston, SC 29403
www.historypress.net

Copyright © 2012 by Sharron Morita
All rights reserved

Front cover, top: A family gathering for lawn games at a house on East Avenue in Bridgeton, circa early 1900s. Courtesy of Jim Bergmann.
Front cover, bottom: Canoe parades and races were regular events in Bridgeton's city park and Tumbling Dam Park in the early decades of the twentieth century. Courtesy of *Claire Biggs*.
Back cover: The center of Bridgeton's downtown, Commerce and Laurel Streets, at the height of the town's golden age in the early 1900s. Courtesy of *Jim Bergmann*.

First published 2012

Manufactured in the United States

ISBN 978.1.60949.527.5

Library of Congress CIP data applied for.

Notice: The information in this book is true and complete to the best of our knowledge. It is offered without guarantee on the part of the author or The History Press. The author and The History Press disclaim all liability in connection with the use of this book.

All rights reserved. No part of this book may be reproduced or transmitted in any form whatsoever without prior written permission from the publisher except in the case of brief quotations embodied in critical articles and reviews.

CONTENTS

ACKNOWLEDGEMENTS

Many individuals have given assistance during the preparation of these pages. They have loaned cherished books, photographs and family memorabilia. They have spent hours in research or given patient answers to anxious queries. They have my gratitude and respect. They are: Jonathan Wood, Cumberland County Historian, for his unfailing kindness toward a nonhistorian; Flavia Alaya, without whom this book would not exist; Jim Bergmann, for the generous loan of photographs and much-valued information; Karen Horwitz, for giving so graciously of her talent; Claire Biggs, Sally Birdsall, Debbi Boykin-Greenberg, Beverly Bradway, Robert Brewer, Ann Budde, Paul Cooper, Mary Caruthers Cossaboon, Arthur Cox, Dean Dellaquila, Maggie DeMarco, Sam Feinstein, Jim Fogle, Sally Garrison, Carola Hartley, Melissa Hemple, Deacon William Johnson, Mary Kimble, Carl Kirstein, Thomas Lane IV, Chris Meyers, Pastor John Norwood, Bonnie Piccioni, Kevin Rabago, Paul Ritter III, James M. Seabrook Jr., Robert Sheldon, Paul Simon, Reverend Richard Sindall, Councilman William Spence, Jean Stelmach, Keith Talbot, Dr. Catherine Tugman, Cesar Viveros, Leonard Wasserman, Penelope S. Watson, Sharon Yoshida, Stanley Kaneshiki and the volunteers at the Seabrook Educational and Cultural Center; Councilman Michael Zapolski Sr., Whitney Tarella, editor at The History Press, and William Estlow, who rescued this technophobe from doing harm to the manuscript; Terri Carpenter, Nereida Pantaleon and Barbara Smith of the Bridgeton Free Public Library staff and Gail Robinson, director of the library; and Warren Q. Adams, director of the Lummis Library.

The Cumberland County seal.

In addition, I am grateful to my husband, Paul, for his help and patient endurance during the months of this revision and to my children, Joe, Katie and Tim, for their encouragement. Most of all, I am grateful to the Holy Spirit for the grace of serendipity that accompanied this project.

Thanks also to the Bridgeton Antiquarian League, especially Joseph DeLuca, for supporting this project and sponsoring the grant application for the book, and to Matt Pisarski of the Cumberland County Cultural and Heritage Commission.

Funding has been made possible in part by the New Jersey Historical Commission/Department of State and the Cumberland County Board of Chosen Freeholders through the Cumberland County Cultural and Heritage Commission.

INTRODUCTION

Bridgeton, New Jersey, is a small town but a complex community nevertheless. It is not one city but many, the disparate parts separated by differences in culture and ethnicity. The story of Bridgeton progresses like the Cohansey River. The river does not follow a straight line. There is no mathematical precision here. The river and the story turn and meander.

The history of Bridgeton is the story of our common ancestors and of the documents and laws that guided them and continue to guide us, and of the events that challenged them and challenge us.

When a book has been in print for twenty-five years, its errors take on the gloss of fact. One aim of this work is to correct the errors of the first edition. For example, scholars have discredited the Wallum Olum, which was thought to be the authentic creation story of the Lenni-Lenape. Despite the purported hoax, it is possible that the document was based on traditional stories, as some tribal members believe. There is no doubt, however, about the error of a statement that worship services were held in local taverns in colonial Cohansey Bridge/Bridgetown. Before the town had its own church, residents attended services in nearby churches, in the courthouse or even outdoors but not in taverns. Also, no evidence supports the assertion that the Cumberland Nail Works ever operated a company store. And finally, although the Ku Klux Klan held very public meetings at Tumbling Dam Park in the 1920s, Klan ownership of the site is not a certainty.

The opportunity to revise a book does not come often. How fortunate is this writer who gets a second chance—to clarify, to correct mistakes, to straighten what was askew, to provide a richer context and deeper understanding than appeared the first time around. So, this work is approached with gratitude.

This book is dedicated to the information and enjoyment of all who read it.

CHAPTER 1

THE ORIGINAL PEOPLE
AND THE SETTLERS

From the beginning, Bridgeton sprouted spontaneously, like a seedling from one of its own oak trees. Nobody founded Bridgeton. No grand design drew the outline of a city. Like many of nature's creations, the town grew up around a body of water, the Cohansey River. The first known structure depended on water for its existence. It was Richard Hancock's sawmill, established in 1686.

But long before the sawmill was built, long before European eyes beheld the forested wilderness of New Jersey, the Bridgeton area was home to the Lenni-Lenape. Tribal history does not reveal the date of their settlement in southern New Jersey. But sometime in the dim past, the whole Algonquin race (of which the Lenni-Lenape were a part) migrated from the western part of the continent to the east. The tribes finally settled along the Delaware, Hudson, Susquehanna and Potomac Rivers.

THE GRANDFATHERS

Tradition, aided by some archaeological evidence, reveals more sparse facts about the Lenni-Lenape. They were peaceful people, at home in the woods and on the water. The local Lenni-Lenape were members of the Unalachtigo branch of the tribe, and they fished, hunted and farmed for their existence. *Unalachtigo* means "people who live by the ocean." *Lenni-Lenape* means "original people" or "men of men." They were revered as the ancestors of all Native Americans. The Nanticoke, their Delaware relatives, called them "grandfathers," a term of respect. Through treaty agreement with the Iroquois, the Lenni-Lenape had adopted a spirit of neutrality. Then

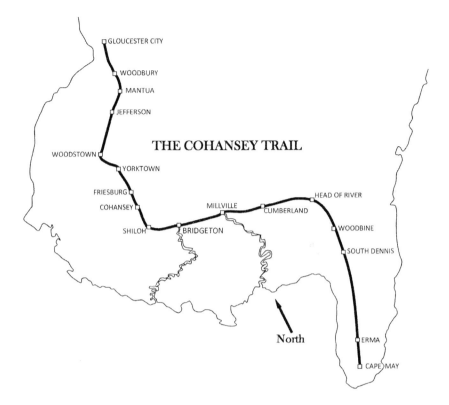

The Cohansey Trail. The map shows the route followed by the Lenni-Lenape and other tribes as they made their way to the ocean and their supply of seafood. *Drawing by Karen Horwitz.*

the fierce Iroquois mocked their peaceable ways and called them "the old women" or "grandmothers."

During the summers, the Unalachtigo and the other tribal groups in what is now called the northeastern United States followed the Cohansey Trail. It was a footpath that connected a point near present-day Gloucester City to Cape May. The trail was one of the major Native American routes that crisscrossed present-day New Jersey.

In the warm season, they harvested the ocean beaches for the conch shells they used for wampum. They also caught and dried fish, clams, crabs and oysters for their winter diet. Their cold-weather inland homes were semi-permanent, used until farming exhausted the fertile soil. Then the Lenni-Lenape families moved on to the next tillable area.

The banks of every stream in the Delaware Bay region have yielded an abundance of arrowheads and pottery fragments, giving proof of the presence of the "original people." Such evidence strongly suggests activity around Jeddy's Pond, East Lake, Sunset Lake and Mary Elmer Lake in Bridgeton. In those days, the lakes did not exist. The Lenni-Lenape found their water in the small streams that would later be dammed to form the lakes.

By the time a group of English Quakers arrived in the Cumberland-Salem area in 1675, native sites in the vicinity of the future Bridgeton had been abandoned. The Cohansey Trail was no longer a tribal thoroughfare. The number of Lenni-Lenape residing in the southern part of the future New Jersey is unknown. European observers estimated the population at about six hundred. The Native Americans kept no statistics, and many of them avoided contact with whites. Their actual number was probably far greater.

Relations between the natives and the new arrivals were peaceful. But the introduction of "civilized diseases," like smallpox and measles, and the European concept of land ownership, unknown to Lenni-Lenape culture, reduced the size of the native population. One Indian said "that for every white man who settled in the area, six Indians died."[1] As the English took over the land, the natives were pushed out.

QUAKER FREEDOM

Conflicting motives inspired the English major John Fenwick to lead a band of Quaker settlers who wanted to establish a colony founded on religious freedom. The Quakers had suffered religious persecution in England. Their refusal to doff their caps to anyone in authority, their pacifism and their religious practice of heeding an inner light did not endear them to their English neighbors. Escape was prudent. They sought and found a land innocent of religious prejudice but rich in unclaimed acres. It was the West Jersey Colony. "It was, in fact, the first Quaker colony in America, antedating Pennsylvania by several years."[2]

The Cohansey area was attractive for several reasons. There was no danger from the Indians. Land could be purchased at fee simple, i.e., it could be bought outright, without leases or quitrents. A quitrent was a fee, sometimes small, but paid regularly and in perpetuity. Prospects for farming were excellent. Cohansey land was much more hospitable to growing crops than the rocky soil of New England. The opportunity to own large swaths of that good land was a strong enticement for the settlers. Such opportunity did not exist back home.

The Quakers persisted despite a government-imposed system that controlled the buying and selling of property and its future management.

That system guaranteed the wrangling and ill will that would follow. It all began in 1664, when King Charles II's brother, James, the Duke of York, granted the lands of New Jersey to Lord John Berkeley and Sir George Carteret. A decade later, Berkeley sold his West Jersey half of the province to John Fenwick and Edward Byllynge (Billing) for £1,000.

The European law of the time permitted appropriation of land in the New World, even though it might be inhabited. West Jersey *was* inhabited—by the Lenni-Lenape, the Nanticoke and some Swedish and Dutch settlers. The Dutch and Swedes did not establish actual settlements in the area but maintained individual farms or trading posts. The Lenni-Lenape were the true residents. The transactions took place in England, and the land was sold, even though neither sellers nor buyers had ever seen it. Some of the sellers never saw their property. And no one consulted the Lenni-Lenape about the land purchases.

THE SALEM TENTH

Fenwick and Byllynge quarreled about their arrangement, and William Penn, who later founded Philadelphia, was asked to mediate. Fenwick was awarded one-tenth of the West Jersey province and Byllynge nine-tenths. Fenwick immediately began to settle his Salem Tenth, which was limited to the area of Salem and Cumberland Counties. But he began his settlement before the Duke of York approved the sale of West Jersey lands. Fenwick had upset the carefully laid plans for the enterprise. His interpretation of governance and landownership kept him embroiled in disputes with fellow Quakers and in legal jeopardy with provincial authorities throughout his life in the colony.

On May 10, 1675, Richard Hancock of Bromley near Bow, Middlesex County, England, an upholsterer, and his wife, Margaret, were issued a patent for five hundred acres of land in Fenwick's Colony, West New Jersey.[3] Proprietor Major John Fenwick issued the patent, and sale was made while they were still in England. Fenwick, Hancock and about one hundred others left on the ship *Griffith*, also known as the *Griffin* or *Griffen*, and landed at Salem on October 4, 1675. This date has been questioned for many years, however, with some historians recording the arrival as early as June 1675.[4] Margaret Hancock remained in England and never saw the new colony.

Fenwick mortgaged his unseen property to fund the *Griffin* and its journey to the unseen territory.[5] This mortgage added to his legal woes, but he forged ahead with his plan to be a land developer.

Ivy Point. John Fenwick built his home on the Delaware River in Salem, New Jersey, in 1677. This eighteenth-century painting depicts the property. *Courtesy of Salem County Historical Society.*

Soon after the arrival of the *Griffin*, Fenwick purchased the land from Oldman's Creek to the Maurice River from the Lenni-Lenape. The natives' ignorance of landownership led to unusual business deals, and they accepted an assortment of goods in return for their wilderness.

FENWICK AND HANCOCK

John Fenwick became governor of the Salem Tenth in June 1676, with Richard Hancock one of the fifteen magistrates. Richard Noble, another settler, was commissioned to be surveyor general. Hancock was deputy surveyor and chief ranger of marshes, swamps and woods. Just two months later, Fenwick discharged Noble from his post for neglect of duty, and Hancock became surveyor general. It is strange that a seventeenth-century upholsterer would possess the mathematical knowledge required for surveying, but Hancock filed returns for more than fifty properties.

As surveyor general, dealing with seemingly limitless tracts of unclaimed land, Richard Hancock may have been tempted to acquire additional land for himself or to otherwise profit from the advantages of his office. He lost favor with Fenwick and was demoted to deputy surveyor. Then Fenwick's son-in-law, Samuel Hedge, became surveyor general. Hancock apparently regained Fenwick's favor and was commissioned a magistrate in 1679, but he lost favor again. If he had recorded all the land he claimed, he would have possessed far more than his allotted five hundred acres, with no way of proving legal ownership.

Fenwick revoked Hancock's commission on December 1, 1680.[6] The evidence points to Fenwick as a difficult, abrasive man. He was not a peaceable Quaker. He ran afoul of the governor of the Dominion of New England, Sir Edmund Andros, and was imprisoned twice. Fenwick was not young when he arrived in West Jersey; he was fifty-seven in 1675. He had been a major in Cromwell's army. So it is no surprise that he retained a military point of view despite his conversion to Quakerism. Perhaps because of that military training, he showed flexibility of mind in his dealings with the Indians. He permitted them to return to the land they had sold to him so they could hunt and fish. This fair treatment could be the reason there were no Indian wars in West Jersey.[7] Fenwick's response was also compatible with the Lenni-Lenape notion of sharing. In their view, the land belonged to the Creator, not to human beings.

From this distance, Fenwick himself cannot be judged fairly. The 1883 Cushing and Sheppard account of his activities states: "It is exceedingly difficult, after the lapse of two hundred years, to form a satisfactory judgment concerning matters wherein so wide a difference of opinion existed at the time." Now, almost four hundred years after Fenwick's birth, and in a culture far removed from his colony, it is even more difficult to do so.

HANCOCK'S MILL

For a time, Hancock seemed to vanish, but he was likely involved in the construction of his dam and sawmill on Mill Creek. Hancock had recorded a survey for himself on September 4, 1676, for 468 acres on Alloways Creek and another unnamed creek. He built a dwelling and outbuildings on the land, which he sold by 1685 before he moved near his mill in Cohansey, later called Bridgeton.

Hancock was an upholsterer, surveyor, ranger and magistrate. He erected one of the first dams in the county and the first sawmill in Cohansey/ Bridgeton. Yet a complete account of his activities and character does not exist. The few early records that mention him reveal property purchases and sales and Fenwick's dismissal of him. But that is hardly an indicator of character. Even the historic sawmill lacked its own deed. Reference to the building first appeared on a survey for another property, so Hancock remains an elusive figure.

It appears he had some education. He was evidently a man of great vitality and initiative and was fearless, for as a surveyor he roamed the wilderness where no European had trod. He married his second wife, Elizabeth Denn, in 1680, and they had a son, Richard, who married Hester Gleaves in 1705. The elder Hancock apparently died in Cohansey/Bridgeton in 1689, though the exact date is unknown.

The exact location of the Hancock sawmill is difficult to pinpoint because small offshoots of the Cohansey River have been dammed and undammed throughout the intervening years. Portions of land now above water were below the waterline in Hancock's day. The mill was perhaps built near the present junction of South Avenue and Grove Street. The mill processed the plentiful cedar timber much in demand for the building of Philadelphia.

The mill was located on the Pamphilia Tract, one of three major tracts that would come together like pieces of a jigsaw puzzle to form Bridgeton. West of the Cohansey River were the Mason and Hutchinson Tracts. The Mason Tract was a five-thousand-acre parcel bought in 1675 by John Mason, a blacksmith of Winchcomb, England. The property covered an area bounded by modern Oak Street at the south end and West Branch of the Cohansey River at the north end. The first building on the tract was a log cabin built in 1697 by John Garrison, who had settled on a Lenni-Lenape clearing near Muddy Run (Jeddy's Pond).

In 1686, a survey of 950 acres was made for Robert Hutchinson, a Burlington Quaker. The northern edge of his property bordered the Mason Tract, and the southern end extended to Cubby Hollow.

THE WEST JERSEY SOCIETY OF BURLINGTON

East of the river, Hancock's mill remained the only settlement for years. In 1693, the West Jersey Society, a land speculation company made up of London businessmen, purchased from Manhaxett and other Native Americans the land between the Cohansey and Maurice Rivers. The area was unknown to the speculators, and they never traveled to see it. John Fenwick had bought this same land upon his arrival in 1675, and he died ten years before this transaction. Because they had no concept of landownership, the Indians often sold land more than once.

This practice prompted the New Jersey legislature to prohibit unauthorized property transactions with Native Americans in the early 1700s. That ruling was made after the West Jersey Society transaction, however. The tract covered eleven thousand acres, most of which remained undeveloped until after Cohansey Bridge (as it would be called) became the county seat.

EARLY SETTLERS

In order to entice the Reverend Thomas Bridge to leave Bermuda to become the pastor of the Fairfield Presbyterian Church in 1695, the West Jersey Society offered Mr. Bridge one thousand acres of the Pamphilia Tract. Bridge became the first land developer in the future town. He had the property surveyed and divided it into forty lots of twenty-five acres each, which he quickly sold. The property became known as the Indian Fields Tract because it had been the location of a Lenni-Lenape settlement and clearing.

Ephraim Seeley settled in the southeastern corner of Bridge's tract. He built a dam across Indian Fields Run, forming the pond known today as East Lake. Water power from the dam generated the first gristmill and fulling mill. Fulling is a process in the making of cloth. The proposed town of Pamphilia never developed, but the name continues in Bridgeton's Pamphylia Avenue.

Thomas Bridge showed keen business sense with his modest development plan. The West Jersey Society and other land speculators sold their properties in much larger blocks, often in thousands of acres. Even settlers of moderate means could afford Bridge's plots in an era when cash was scarce. The Indian Fields Tract became the first permanent settlement in the Bridgeton vicinity.

Bridge's business plan fit well with West Jersey. It was a yeoman society.[8] The colony was home to small- and medium-sized farms, and the owners worked the land themselves. There were few absentee landlords, and there were "relatively few indentured servants in West Jersey."[9] There were no cash crops like tobacco, rice or indigo, which were grown in other colonies. But there was no hunger or privation; farm families could subsist on the crops they grew.

A REMARKABLE DOCUMENT

The Quakers came to West Jersey for its farmland, it is true. But they also came to establish a colony based on Quaker principles. To that end, they created the groundbreaking charter called the Concessions and Agreements of 1676/7. They retained an English sense of fairness and justice, and they wanted their colony to maintain the liberties embedded in English law. They added their own capacity for tolerance, honed by their experience with prejudice in England. The effort to devise their own system of law occurred in Burlington, in Byllynge's Nine-Tenths, away from John Fenwick, with William Penn as one of the contributors. The resulting document continues to be heralded and studied as a model charter. In Chapter XVI of the Concessions, complete religious freedom is proclaimed:

> *That no men, nor number of men upon earth, hath power or authority to rule over men's consciences in religious matters; therefore it is consented, agreed and ordained, that no person or persons whatsoever, within the said province, at any time or times hereafter shall be any ways, upon any pretence whatsoever, called in question, or in the least punished or hurt, either in person, estate or privilege, for the sake of his opinion, judgment, faith or worship towards God, in matters of religion.*

The Concessions placed power in an assembly elected by "proprietors, freeholders and inhabitants." This contrasted with the inherited power of the English monarch. Members of the assembly received a shilling in payment for their work. The document declared that because they received payment, even if only a shilling, from the people, assembly members were servants of those people. The Concessions included the right to a public trial by jury for every person, as well as a provision for assembly meetings open to all. Taxes could not be levied without consent of the people. This excellent document was not put to full use, however.

The Duke of York undermined its force. He named the absent Byllynge as governor of West Jersey, and Byllynge in turn named as deputy governor Samuel Jennings of Buckinghamshire. The Concessions had not even mentioned the office of governor; all power was vested in the assembly. Jennings traveled to West Jersey and acceded to the demands of the colonists for the rights of the assembly. But even with a benevolent deputy governor, it was apparent that the purpose of the Concessions had been thwarted.[10]

Chapter XXIII of the Concessions prohibited slavery in West Jersey, but the law was not enforced and slavery did exist there. Slavery was legal and practiced more widely in East Jersey at the time. The humane Quaker influence expressed so firmly and eloquently in the Concessions diminished further when West and East Jersey were forcibly merged into the Royal Colony of New Jersey in 1702. After that, royal authority superseded all colonial law.

The number of slaves in seventeenth-century West Jersey is unknown. But the presence and number of slaves in the eighteenth and nineteenth centuries in the area is documented.[11] They tended to be house servants rather than field hands. An 1889 account of Bridgeton states matter-of-factly:

> *Up to the year 1800 there were a number of slaves in Bridgeton, black persons being held as chattel in New Jersey. In 1804 the Legislature passed an act for the gradual abolition of slavery, so that the number thereafter decreased continually. In 1830 there were still two persons owned as slaves, but with their death emancipation in the State became complete.*[12]

In Cumberland County in 1790, there were 120 slaves; in 1800, 75; in 1810, 42; in 1820, 28; in 1830, the 2 mentioned above. The gradual abolition prescribed by the 1804 law did not apply to current slaves; they were slaves until they died. The law applied only to slave children born after July 4, 1804. A daughter would achieve freedom on her twenty-first birthday and a son on his twenty-fifth. A law calling for complete abolition was not passed until 1846. With that legislation, New Jersey became the last northern state to abolish slavery.

CHAPTER 2
CONNECTING THE SETTLEMENTS

S mall homes and businesses sprang up near the river, and a bridge was needed. Travelers crossed the river at a fording place, and a bridge would improve the journey considerably. So in 1716, Seth Brooks, a carpenter of Cohansey, built "the Great Bridge over Cohansie Creek." It was the first span over the Cohansey River and was built in the area of the modern Commerce Street Bridge. Log pens or cribs were sunk into the water and filled with rocks to provide a solid foundation. The structure was very narrow and could not be opened to permit boats to proceed up the river. Frequently during tides that were higher than normal, the water rose above the level of the bridge floor. This caused great inconvenience, particularly for anyone attempting to lead horses or cattle to the other side of the river. A deposition made in 1739 by Brooks provides a description:[13]

> *Seth Brooks of Cohansie in the County of Salem and the Western Division of the Providence of New Jersey, Carpenter, (aged fifty years or thereabouts) maketh oath, saithe this Dep*[osition] *at the time he built the Great Bridge over Cohansie Creek with log pens which is now two or three and twenty* [years] *ago, went to face a certain white oak tree which is since rotted down but the stump still remains, in order to make a log for the said Bridge, which said tree stood above a little cover which is about twelve or fifteen rod above the dwelling House of Elias Cotting near the said creek.*

With the bridge came more activity. Local inhabitants began to call the surrounding area "Cohansey Bridge." The modest span linked the tiny settlements on either side of the Cohansey River and provided an alternative to the ferry that plied between Greenwich and Fairfield. Repairs were made

Rulon Brooks Sr. built this model of the first bridge over the Cohansey River to commemorate Bridgeton's 300th anniversary in 1986. Brooks was the fifth great-grandson of Seth Brooks, who built the span around 1716. Early descriptions of the bridge served as a guide in construction of the model. *Photo by Flavia Alaya.*

from time to time, and the bridge was probably widened to permit use by wagons or carriages. By 1774, the "Great Bridge" needed major repairs or replacement. When the condition of the bridge deteriorated, some residents argued to abandon it and build a new span at the end of Broad Street. One of the main opponents of this plan was Alexander Moore, a shopkeeper and landowner. Between 1730 and 1740, he built the first store in the small settlement, on the northeast corner of Commerce and Cohansey Streets, and traffic from the bridge passed right by his establishment. But Moore had more than business in mind. He had a plan for a town called Cumberland.

ALEXANDER MOORE

If Bridgeton needs to name a founder, Alexander Moore deserves the title more than anyone in its history. He was born in 1704, of Irish descent, and arrived in the Cohansey area about 1730. Near his general store he built a substantial home that served as a tavern for many years after his death. During his lifetime, he accumulated 3,000 acres of land, and in 1752, he purchased 990 acres of that total on the east side of the river. He paid the West Jersey Society £247 for the property.

In 1754, he hired surveyor Daniel Elmer Jr. to plot out the proposed town on the newly acquired tract. The tract included Jefferson Street (now East Broad Street) at the south and Washington Street at the north end, with the river as the west boundary and Orange Street at the east line. Moore's plan was orderly. The streets were at right angles, forming squares of 2.14 acres each. Moore never realized his plan, but the property eventually became the first and second wards of Bridgeton. In Moore's day, most of the land was still virgin forest.

Conditions for development were favorable. On January 19, 1747/8,[14] the New Jersey legislature created the county of Cumberland from the eastern part of Salem County. The new county was named for the Duke of Cumberland, who, in 1746, defeated the Pretender Charles Edward Stuart (Bonnie Prince Charlie) at the Battle of Culloden in Scotland. Courts for the new county were held at Cohansey Bridge, so the settlement enjoyed some government-imposed stability.

In 1760, the royal governor and his council appointed Moore as one of the judges of the Court of Common Pleas, an appointment he held until July 4, 1776. After the U.S. Constitution was adopted, he was elected to be a judge and retired because of failing health at the end of the five-year term.

In October 1747, Moore married Sarah Reeves, the daughter of Abraham Reeves, a deacon of the Greenwich Presbyterian Church. They had five children: Sarah, born August 21, 1748; Ann, born September 8, 1753; Alexander Jr., born August 30, 1754; and two children who died in infancy. Sarah married John White, an English merchant of Philadelphia. She died in 1770, at the age of twenty-two, after bearing three sons, Alexander, William and John Moore White, who became a leader of the community. Moore's other daughter, Ann, married Dr. Isaac Harris of Pittsgrove Township. During the Revolutionary War, he was a surgeon in General Newcomb's brigade.

Alexander Moore Jr. married a Miss Tate and lived on a farm west of Bridgetown on property now occupied by the Cumberland Manor, the county nursing home. Sometime after his wife died in 1775, Alexander Sr. moved to the farm, where he spent his remaining years. He died on September 5, 1786, leaving the bulk of his estate of over £6,000 to Alexander Jr. and the property east of the bridge to daughter Sarah's children. He also left a £50 bequest for the construction of a Presbyterian church in Bridgetown. Alexander and Sarah Moore were members of the Greenwich Presbyterian Church and were buried in the church cemetery.

HOPE FOR CUMBERLAND TOWN

Alexander Moore's town of Cumberland never materialized, but John Moore White clung to his grandfather's hopes. He inherited some of

Alexander's east Bridgetown property and acquired the remainder of the unsold portion from his brothers and began improvements. White sold lots from the property and rerouted the road to Deerfield to create the present North Laurel Street from Commerce Street to near North Street. Later, he redirected several blocks of Pearl Street and Irving Avenue.

He commissioned a town plan with a street layout for the entire property, but few of the streets were ever opened. When White opened a law practice in Bridgetown in 1791, he built an imposing house at Commerce and Laurel Streets. The mansion later became part of the Davis Hotel, a gathering place for local society.

White maintained his grandfather's interest in the "Great Bridge." He wanted a drawbridge built to replace the old one and got his wish in 1799. He also wanted to erect wharves above the bridge, but wharves would be useless with a stationary bridge. He won the county freeholders to his view when he offered to assume the cost of the draw and keep it in good repair for five years. He also deeded river property for a free landing to a group of trustees. Years later, he reclaimed the land by asserting that terms of the trust had been broken. In 1808, White left Bridgetown for Woodbury, where he continued the practice of law. Later, he became a justice of the New Jersey Supreme Court.

John Moore White's home at the corner of Commerce and Laurel Streets, built in 1791, later became the Davis Hotel, shown in 1876. *Courtesy of the Cumberland County Historical Society, from 1876* Historical Atlas of Cumberland County.

Moore and White brought order to the unformed development of Bridgetown. When White left for Woodbury, a town had begun to emerge from the virgin forest of cedar, oak and pine.

INNKEEPERS AND CRAFTSMEN

In the mid-1700s, a small group of craftsmen and businesspeople tried to wrest a livelihood from Cohansey Bridge. A few opened taverns or inns in their homes. Travelers going east from Salem to Cape May, or west to Salem and Philadelphia, or between Greenwich and Fairfield, used the main road through Cohansey Bridge. An inn was a welcome respite from hard travel. Inns were more than places of refreshment. They were the social and political centers of a town. The known business owners and their periods of activity included:

SILAS PARVIN, who built a two-story, hip-roofed house at the corner of Commerce and Atlantic Streets, near the back of the present Woodruff's Paint Store. At that time, Commerce Street ended just west of the bridge and did not continue directly up the hill, but a road ran from the foot of the bridge diagonally up the hill to where the courthouse stood in the middle of Broad Street. Silas Parvin received his first license to keep a tavern in 1737 and renewed the license, usually every year until 1763. He died in 1779.

JEREMIAH SAYRE, a shoemaker (cordwainer), owned a house near the present courthouse. A cordwainer made and repaired boots, shoes, leather harnesses, aprons and buckets. Leather buckets were considered lighter and more durable than wooden ones.

JOHN HALL, a blacksmith, had a home on the site of the modern county courthouse, with a forge built just west of it. He, too, was licensed to keep a tavern in his home. The house caught fire and burned with most of his possessions, and the fire spread to the courthouse. Historians differ on the date of the fire. Some say it was December 1758 and others January 3, 1759. Hall rebuilt his home and obtained another tavern license in December 1759, which he held until 1766.

With the flow of traffic steadily increasing because of the bridge over the Cohansey, CAPTAIN ELIAS COTTING, a sea captain from Boston, saw the financial rewards of providing bed and board for travelers. In 1739, he acquired a tavern license and opened an inn in his house built right on the river near Broad Street. Like all tavern owners, Cotting was required to guarantee that his inn "had at least two good spare feather beds more than was necessary for his own family and was well provided with meat and drink for the accommodation of man and stabling and provinder for horses."[15] The Cotting place was probably as convenient for those coming to Cohansey Bridge by boat as it was to those traveling on foot or horseback. Until the courthouse was built in 1752, cases were often heard in the Cotting and Parvin taverns. Cotting was the first clerk of Cumberland County, appointed by Governor Belcher in 1748. He held the position until his death in 1757.

The house of BENJAMIN SAYRE stood near the Parvin tavern. The nature of Sayre's craft or business remains unknown, and the house was sold in 1766 to settle Sayre's debts.[16]

JOHN GARRISON built the first house west of the river in 1697 on the north side of Jeddy's Pond, on the property known as the Park Farm in the twentieth century, where the Little League field is now located. A romantic story concerning Garrison and his wife has persisted through the years and has been recounted in news articles and books. However, no conclusive proof exists to determine the truth or fiction of the tale. Mrs. Sarah Smith, in an interview in an 1843 issue of the *Bridgeton Chronicle*, reprinted in New Jersey Historical Collections by John W. Barber and Henry Howe, reported:

> *Her great-grandmother Elizabeth, in the troublous times of that kingdom, was compelled to flee from her native country, [Sweden], when she was sixteen years old. She was concealed in a hogshead, on board of a ship, at Stockholm, for some time before the vessel sailed for America. She brought many valuable treasures with her across the water, which were also concealed on board the ship; but after the vessel had sailed over the Atlantic, she was wrecked on the Jersey shore. This lady, with a few of the crew, barely saved their lives. In her destitute condition, on the shore of a vast wilderness, as New Jersey then was, she fell in with a hunter by the name of Garrison. Their acquaintance grew into intimacy, and ripened into love. She married him, and by him had ten children. It is said that her youngest son, William, was born in her fifty-fifth year. She died in the ninety-fifth year of her age.*

Mrs. Smith's great-grandmother, Elizabeth, was reputed to be a Swedish princess.

The six properties described above were in what was then known as Hopewell Township on the western side of the Cohansey River. For the next fifty years, most of the homes and businesses were built there, near the courthouse. No deeds were issued for properties east of the river until Alexander Moore purchased his 990 acres. But homes and businesses, including Moore's general store, were built without the benefit of deeds.

ACROSS THE RIVER

In 1750, there were few homes or businesses on the east side of the river. Isaac Smith owned a home near the present intersection of Broad and Laurel Streets, with a wharf adjoining. Smith also kept a tavern where the court convened in 1748.

Ephraim Seeley owned grist- and fulling mills on the site of the present East Lake, with the Seeley "mansion-house" nearby.[17]

On the brow of a hill in the East Avenue neighborhood was John Keen's home, which served as a tavern from 1754 to 1775. A special meeting of justices and freeholders was held there the morning after the courthouse fire in 1758 (or 1759).

In 1748, Richard Hancock's sawmill and an adjacent house were still standing, owned and occupied by Colonel Enos Seeley. The east side of the river remained mostly open woods until after the Revolutionary War.

These were the principal structures in the Cohansey Bridge of 1748, a place with a population of fifty to seventy-five persons, all of whom could have fit into the new courthouse without crowding it.

CHAPTER 3

THE SPIRIT OF REVOLUTION

In the middle of the eighteenth century, Cohansey Bridge was a sleepy hamlet. The village of Greenwich was the busiest, most populated settlement in the new county. Residents of Cohansey Bridge traveled there and to Philadelphia for supplies. Presbyterian, Baptist, Quaker and Episcopal congregations had already built churches in or around Greenwich. Deerfield and Fairfield had Presbyterian churches. Cohansey Bridge had none. Worshippers met in the courthouse for services, journeyed to the established churches or "met in the open air, under the trees."[18] By the 1740s, Quakers were outnumbered by the Presbyterians and Baptists from New England and Long Island they had invited to their West Jersey colony decades earlier. The number of Quakers had diminished, mostly because many of them had married "out of meeting."

With "Cumberland" chosen as the name of the new county, residents indicated pro-British, pro–House of Hanover sentiment. But that loyalty would sour into opposition over the next twenty-five years.

When Cumberland became a county, the first courts were held in Greenwich, the temporary county seat. But Cohansey Bridge became the permanent county seat after it was chosen by a vote of county residents in 1749, and court was moved there. Cohansey Bridge was closer to the center of the county than Greenwich and, therefore, a better location. The focus of commerce and politics then shifted from Greenwich to Cohansey Bridge. The name of the town changed gradually to Bridgetown by 1765.

For a time, a gaol (jail) was maintained wherever a sheriff happened to live, so the jail remained in Greenwich, the home of Sheriff Ananias Sayre. The gaol measured twelve square feet, about the size of a flimsy corncrib. Prisoners escaped from it regularly. In 1754, the gaol was abandoned for one in Cohansey Bridge.

COURTHOUSE ON THE HILL

In 1750, the county freeholders instructed Richard Wood and Ebenezer Miller, Greenwich justices of the peace, to raise money for a courthouse and jail. Miller was appointed despite the fact that he owned a debated title to the property on which both buildings would be erected. He and Wood assessed taxes called "certainties," levied to pay only for the buildings. Revenue for the small frame courthouse (thirty-two feet by twenty-two feet, two stories high) totaled £320. The contractor was Howell Powell, a future sheriff, and court opened on August 25, 1752, though the building was unfinished. The courthouse was built at the end of Broad Street, and when the roadway was extended, the building was then in the middle of the street.

In the winter of 1758–59 (between December 6 and January 4), when John Hall's tavern next to the courthouse caught fire, flames spread to the courthouse, and it burned to the ground. Soon after the fire, the justices of the peace and freeholders held a special meeting at John Keen's tavern. They

The only known likeness of General Ebenezer Elmer. He and his brother, Jonathan, were physicians and Revolutionary War–era leaders in Bridgetown. *Courtesy of Cumberland County Historical Society.*

decided that a brick courthouse should be built to replace the ruined wooden structure. The new building would be no larger than the old, but it would have eighteen-inch-thick walls on the first floor and a cupola on the roof. Once again, county residents were assessed a special tax to pay for the courthouse.

Since Cohansey Bridge/Bridgetown had no churches at the time, the courthouse was used for religious services on Sundays and weekdays. The courthouse hill was steep, and every heavy rain eroded the earth along the foundation. The situation demanded repairs by 1766, but the building continued to serve the public until 1844.

Wherever residents gathered, they spoke against the British and their despised taxes, especially the tea tax. Opposition to the British was not unanimous;

there were Tories in the neighborhood too. Richard Cayford, a tavern keeper of Bridgetown who also operated a stagecoach from Bridgetown to Cooper's Ferry, was an outspoken Tory who became a British officer.[19] Dr. Ebenezer Elmer, also of Bridgetown, kept a journal that relates the high feelings and eventual preparations against the crown: "Committee met at courthouse, met to choose…officers for militia…Day appointed as a Continental fast… Exercised at John Dare's [tavern], had firing, Richard Howell a beating up for volunteers; got many."[20]

THE TEA BURNERS

The first Continental Congress of the colonies met in Philadelphia on September 5, 1774. Colonists pledged not to import or use merchandise from Great Britain, including tea from the East India Tea Company. That December, the brig *Greyhound* sailed up the Cohansey River to Greenwich with a cargo of tea bound for Philadelphia. The ship docked secretly, for fear of public outcry, and the tea was stored in a Greenwich cellar. Ten days later, county residents held an already scheduled general meeting in Bridgetown. The meeting supported the conclusions of the Continental Congress and appointed a committee of thirty-five to execute the results on the county level. The committee planned to meet the next morning to discuss the matter of the Greenwich tea.

That night, however, a group of men, all disguised as Indians, seized the tea and burned it in Greenwich's market square. The committee of thirty-five expressed disapproval of the destruction and vowed no legal protection for those responsible, despite the fact that some of its members were tea burners.

The owners of the tea filed suit against the tea burners in April 1775. Joseph Bloomfield, a Bridgetown attorney, and Jonathan Sergeant, a Philadelphia lawyer, represented the defendants. Money for the defense was raised by subscription. The owners named Alexander Moore Jr., Henry Seeley, Richard Howell, Joel Miller, Ephraim Newcomb, Abraham Sheppard and Silas Newcomb as tea burners. When he was in his eighties, Ebenezer Elmer claimed that he was one of the tea burners. He added the names of David Pierson, Stephen Pierson, Silas Whittaker, Timothy Elmer, Andrew Hunter Jr., Philip Vickers Fithian, Clarence Parvin, John Hunt, Lewis Howell, Henry Stacks, James Ewing, Thomas Ewing, Joel Fithian and Josiah Seeley. There is no way to verify the accuracy of either list.

Joseph Reed of Newcastle, Delaware, and a Mr. Pettit of Burlington were attorneys for the owners, John Duffield and Stacey Hepburn. The owners failed to file security for costs, and the case was closed the following year. It was briefly reopened but closed again when the colonies broke with royal authority.

Even though the civil suit failed, the court attempted to have the tea burners indicted in 1775. Chief Justice Frederick Smyth charged the grand jury to indict the tea burners, but the jury did nothing, and court broke up. Judge Smyth sent the jury out a second time, again with no results. Dr. Jonathan Elmer, brother of Ebenezer, was the sheriff, and he had summoned a jury of Whigs. (Whigs supported colonial independence. Tories favored continued government by the British.)

DR. JONATHAN ELMER

When Elmer's term as sheriff expired in June 1775, New Jersey governor William Franklin appointed David Bowen, a Tory supporter, to replace him. Even a Tory sheriff could not succeed in bringing an indictment against the defendants, and that ended the case. But Dr. Elmer's career as a public servant had just begun. He remains one of the most outstanding figures in local history. He was certainly Bridgetown's most politically influential and greatly respected citizen before, during and after the Revolution.

Jonathan Elmer was born in Cedarville in 1745. He endured frail health from an early age, yet he managed to live a lifetime of considerable achievement that would exhaust a person in perfect health. He was a member of the first graduating class of the Medical Department of the University of Pennsylvania of 1771. Dr. Benjamin Rush praised his medical acumen. Rush said, "In medical knowledge he was exceeded by no physician in the United States." Dr. Elmer returned to Bridgetown to practice medicine, but the constant horseback travel required of a country physician proved too much for him. Though he did not maintain an active medical practice, he continued to treat some patients and to consult with other doctors. Perhaps his stay in Philadelphia as a medical student had inspired patriotic fervor, for he soon entered politics.

In addition to serving as sheriff of Cumberland County, he became a member of the county Committee of Observation in 1774, and in 1775, he was chosen to be a deputy to the Provincial Congress. These two bodies were precursors to the Continental Congress, for which Elmer was a delegate in 1776, 1777–78 and 1781–83. He was elected to the legislative council of New Jersey in 1780 and again in 1784. In 1788, he was a member of the

Congress under the Articles of Confederation, and he became a senator under the new United States Constitution. In Cumberland County, he served as clerk, surrogate, freeholder, justice of the peace and common pleas judge. During the Revolutionary War, he was a member of Congress and served on the medical committee to oversee military hospitals.

In 1787, he was elected president of the Medical Society of New Jersey. He was presiding elder of the Broad Street Presbyterian Church. In 1774, he had been selected for membership in the American Philosophical Society, an honorary society founded by Benjamin Franklin. That prestigious society continues to this day. In 1769, he married Mary Seeley, daughter of Colonel Ephraim Seeley. They had eight children, four of whom died in infancy. Dr. Elmer died in 1817.

He spoke and wrote eloquently about the tyranny of the English Parliament regarding taxation of the colonies and the importance of political freedom. In an address to the inhabitants of Cumberland County in May 1775, he said:

> *The cause we are engaged in is good. We are only contending for our constitutional rights & privileges & that Liberty wherewith God hath made us free, & may he enable us to persevere therein with unshaken resolution till we gain the point. For we are actually reduced to the horid* [sic] *alternative either to acknowledge ourselves tenants at will to the British parliament or resolutely oppose them & matters seem to have gone so far that unless we tamely submit a civil war must inevitably ensue.*[21]

THE ROLE OF TAVERNS

In the days before the Revolution, Bridgetown was a village with no more than 150 residents, representing perhaps twenty-five to thirty households, and several taverns. To the colonial man, the local tavern was far more than a place where he could quench his thirst. It was his club, the place where local happenings were discussed and, in the days before a local newspaper, the source of information from other communities.

The title of innkeeper carried a certain social distinction. Innkeepers were the best-informed and most widely acquainted men in town. Excerpts from a petition for the licensing of a tavern give an idea of the importance of the position:

> *We the subscriber freeholders and inhabitants of the Township of Hopewell, believing that a public inn or Tavern to be necessary for the transaction of*

publick business, and will be conducive to publick good for the accomodation
of travelers, do recommend this man as a suitable person to keep said Inn or
Tavern, that he is a man of good repute for honesty and sobriety.[22]

Water was rarely used as a beverage. The common drink was hard cider, which had an alcoholic content equal to that of beer. Cider was available in taverns and was made in homes as well. The journal of clergyman Philip Vickers Fithian records that 750 gallons of cider were made by the Fithians in a single season. In addition, fifteen barrels of ciderkin—a weaker cider made for children—were made from the mast left in the cider press after the first squeezing.[23]

Rum and imported wines were stocked by every general store for the convenience of the housewife. The tavern was obviously more than a source of liquid spirits. Common beverages were easily obtained elsewhere, but the conviviality of the public house offered a more stimulating brew.

A TAVERN KEEPER OF NOTE

Matthew Potter was the most celebrated innkeeper of Bridgetown. He was born in 1734 in Ulster, Ireland, where his father, a Scotsman from Edinburgh, was engaged in the linen trade. Soon after Matthew's birth, Irish industries began to suffer from restrictions placed on them by the British government. The Potters, with sons Matthew, James and John, immigrated to Connecticut in 1740. They soon moved to Philadelphia, where another son, David, was born in 1745. Matthew and David eventually moved to Bridgetown. Matthew opened a blacksmith shop and kept a tavern in his home. David became a merchant dealing in grain, produce and lumber, growing so prosperous that he shipped goods to market in his own vessels.

Matthew Potter's home-tavern was on the north side of Broad Street, just opposite the entrance to the courthouse. It was "the principal inn of the town."[24] In 1775, it had become the favorite gathering place for young men of the leading families of the area. Among the habitués were some of the tea burners of the Greenwich incident and the man who defended them in court, Joseph Bloomfield.

Potter's Tavern became a landmark of historic America because of a public notice posted throughout the area on December 21, 1775. The notice began:

As the circumstances of the times loudly call for every Individual to exert
himself for the good of his Country and fellow creatures, several persons

Potter's Tavern, the location of the posting of the *Plain Dealer*, sometimes called New Jersey's first newspaper, though it was more opinion than news. The tavern has been restored to its eighteenth-century appearance. *Photo by Sam Feinstein.*

> *whose genius & inclination for many years past have led them to Study and contemplation, have concluded, that the most Important Service that they can render to Society, will be to communicate—Weekly to their neighbors the result of their enquiries and Speculations on political occurrances and other important Subjects particularly calculated to suit this place.*[25]

THE *PLAIN DEALER*

Thus was born the *Plain Dealer*. The would-be journalists had no printing press, so they alternated as copiers of the essays. The newsletter was available for reading at Potter's Tavern each Tuesday morning. Interested persons could copy the material and take it home if they wished, but the authors would remain anonymous, "without the inconvenience of being known or personally critecised."[26]

The aim of the newsletter was "to imitate the *Spectator* and other London publications, which in polished essays cleverly hit off the foibles of the day. To this was added the more serious purpose of arousing and stimulating the patriotism of the people."[27]

Copies of eight issues of the *Plain Dealer* have survived and are preserved in the rare book collection of the Rutgers University Library. The anonymity of the authors has persisted, and historians can only speculate about the origin of the essays. The editor was probably Ebenezer Elmer, a twenty-three-year-old native of Fairfield, the confessed tea burner. He was a physician who later distinguished himself as a soldier and statesman. Most likely, Elmer was the author of the eulogy of General Montgomery, which appeared in the seventh number of the newsletter, in which was stated:

> *Arouse my countrymen! Let the memory of our departed hero, doubly animate us, with courage, and resolution to defend our liberties, and avenge his death! Let us draw our swords, and never return them into their scabboards, till we have rescued our Country, from the Iron hand of Tyranny, And secured the pure enjoyment of Liberty, to generations yet unborn!*

Joseph Bloomfield, Richard and Lewis Howell and Dr. Jonathan Elmer were likely writers too. It is possible that the eight existing issues constitute the total run of the newsletter. The crush of events leading to the Revolution of 1776 no doubt demanded the attention of the contributors, to the exclusion of writing weekly essays. The final issue appeared in February 1776.

Although the *Plain Dealer* was a high-minded publication, the writers devoted more than a little space to the quaint courting ritual known as "bundling." The discussion ignited a vehement response from pro- and anti-bundling adherents. The *Plain Dealer* has been called the first regular newspaper in New Jersey, but it delivered opinions rather than news. Whether it was a newspaper or opinion broadsheet, it was brave and important in influence and purpose.

Because he permitted the *Plain Dealer* to be displayed and read in his bar, Matthew Potter placed himself in danger in the days preceding the Revolution, situated as he was opposite the door of the courthouse. It was a symbol of the laws and policies of King George III. The stocks and pillory near the north end of the courthouse were a constant reminder of the punishments imposed on transgressors of those laws.

Colonel David Potter, Matthew's brother, built a large combination dwelling and store on the corner of Franklin and Broad Streets in 1780. This building was demolished in 1966 to make way for a service station. Potter's Tavern was

The Bridgeton Liberty Bell rang out the independence of the colonies in August 1776. It is kept in the Cumberland County Courthouse. *Photo by Sam Feinstein.*

eventually converted into a two-family home and permitted to deteriorate to an advanced state. It was saved from demolition, mainly through the efforts of the late J. Meade Landis, a local historian, and purchased by the City of Bridgeton in 1958. Currently, it is maintained by the Cumberland County Board of Freeholders and hosted by the Cumberland County Historical Society.

Though Bridgetown was far removed from military action of the rebellion, it voiced the sentiments of the Revolution when independence was declared in Philadelphia. Bridgetown's own Liberty Bell, housed in the cupola atop the courthouse, rang out in honor of the declaration.

INDEPENDENCE DECLARED

When a courier from Philadelphia announced the news in August 1776,

> *the officers of the militia and a great number of other inhabitants having met at Bridgetown went in procession to the courthouse, where the declaration of independence, the Constitution of New Jersey and the Treason Ordinance were publicly read and approved of. These were followed by a spirited*

address by Dr. Jonathan Elmer, Chairman of the Committee, after which the King's Coat of Arms were burned in the street. The Affair was conducted with the greatest decency and regularity.[28]

In his spirited address, Elmer urged responsible and unselfish citizenship on his listeners. He waited until the New Jersey Constitution had been adopted before delivering his speech. New Jersey now had a set of laws firmly in place, and he wanted his audience to know that independence did not mean the end of the rule of law. His speech bears repeating:

No people under Heaven, were ever favored with a fairer opportunity, of laying a sure foundation for future grandeur and happiness than we. The plan of government established in most states and kingdoms of the world, has been the effect of chance or necessity, ours of sober reason and cool deliberation, our future happiness or misery therefore, as a people, will depend entirely upon ourselves.

If actuated by principles of virtue and genuine patriotism, we make the welfare of our country the sole aim of all our actions; If we entrust none but persons of abilities and integrity, with the management of our public affairs; If we carefully guard against corruption and undue influence, in the several departments of government; If we are steady and zealous in putting the laws in strict execution; the spirit and principles of our new constitution, which we have just now heard read, may be preserved for a long time; but if faction and party spirit, the destruction of popular governments, take place, anarchy and confusion will soon ensue.

The constitution he referred to was the newly adopted New Jersey Constitution, which he had helped to draft. The previous month, British troops had arrived in New York to quash the rebellion and finish the hostilities begun at Lexington and Concord. But fighting continued until the surrender of General Cornwallis at Yorktown in 1781.

During the war years, the Elmer brothers played their parts, Ebenezer as a regimental surgeon in the Continental army and Jonathan as a member of Congress. No battles were fought in Bridgetown or anywhere in Cumberland County. However, British soldiers did forage for livestock and food along the Delaware Bay, as close as Bacon's Neck in Greenwich Township, and Tory farmers probably sold supplies to the British.

CHAPTER 4

AFTER THE WAR

The fifty years following the Revolutionary War were years of dramatic change and growth. The Industrial Revolution brought heavy industries that overshadowed the original saw- and gristmills. A major bank opened its doors, and new roads and public transportation connected Bridgetown with the wider world. The new roads, leading to other villages and the county's lower townships, greatly increased travel and trade. Vital services and supplies became available locally. Residents no longer needed to travel by horseback or boat to Greenwich or Salem for supplies. They could furnish their homes and provide for their families with resources from Bridgetown. At least four stage lines provided service to and from the town. A community began to coalesce around a church, schools, manufacturing and a bank.

THE FIRST CHURCH

Although freedom of religion was a factor in the settlement of West Jersey, the residents of Bridgetown did not build their first church until the 1790s. Alexander Moore had bequeathed property at Commerce and Pearl Streets and £50 for the construction of a Presbyterian church, but members of the proposed church disagreed about its location. Mark Miller, a Quaker, donated two acres of land on Broad Street, with other contributors eventually increasing the size to twenty acres. Cash donations totaled £600. But the Revolutionary War halted the project. Building then commenced in the spring of 1792 but stopped in December when the money ran out. Dr. Ebenezer Elmer, then a member of the New Jersey Assembly, obtained legislative approval for a fundraising scheme, a lottery, which provided the needed funds. Churches

Old Broad Street Church, as it appears now, with Broad Street School in the background, was built in 1792–95. The congregation of First Presbyterian Church uses Old Broad Street Church for services in August every year. The front of the church faces away from Broad Street. *Photo by Reverend Richard Sindall.*

often used such lotteries to raise money: "The lottery method of raising money in those days was considered entirely honorable, and nothing was thought of it."[29] The new church was dedicated in May 1795. Less than five years later, the state passed a law prohibiting such lotteries.

The original road between Bridgetown and Greenwich passed south of the church. The side that faces Broad Street was considered the back of the church.

The Broad Street Presbyterian Church continued its unusual history when it became the scene of a murder trial in 1797. John Patterson, alias Robert Brown, an Irish seaman, was accused of killing the captain, Andrew Conrow, and wounding two crew members aboard a rigger in the Maurice River near present-day Port Norris. The courthouse was too small to hold the crowd anxious to attend the trial, so the church was used. Some avid spectators viewed the proceedings from the church rafters. Patterson was found guilty, mainly due to the testimony of a cabin boy who hid in the ship's sails out of fear. The fear was justified because Patterson tried to choke the boy during the trial. The defendant was found guilty and sentenced to be hanged, but he hanged himself the first night he was confined to the county jail.

In 1758, the first execution in the county had taken place on what would later be the church grounds. Francis Pickering, alias Mason, alias Price, was arrested for stealing a horse and mare, tried and convicted and sentenced to be hanged on a common on Broad Street. The site is now part of the Broad Street Church cemetery.

THE FIRST SCHOOLS

Universal education was not the norm. Church groups frequently operated schools in order that members might learn to read the Bible. Education was a sporadic enterprise before the establishment of the Broad Street Church and other churches. Some fortunate children were educated at home by their parents or by paid tutors. Ministers often served as tutors, as was the case for Dr. Jonathan Elmer when he was a boy in Cedarville. Young Jonathan was the pupil of his grandfather, the Reverend Daniel Elmer, the pastor of the Cohansey Presbyterian Church in Fairfield. When his grandfather died, Jonathan attended the school of the Reverend William Ramsay, who had a profound influence on young Elmer's thinking.[30]

Formal education in Bridgetown began with John Westcott's private school in 1773. Reading, writing and mathematics were the preferred

Brearley Lodge as it appeared in 1797. The Bank Street building was the site of a Masonic Lodge and the Harmony Academy, one of Bridgeton's early schools. Lodge members continue to use the building for their meetings. *Courtesy of Brearley Lodge.*

subjects. In 1780, Andrew Hunter, a Princeton classmate of Philip Vickers Fithian, opened a classical school for boys on Broad Street. The students probably studied Latin and Greek, since those subjects were a foundation for college preparation.

Around 1792, Mark Miller, the benefactor of the Broad Street Church, also donated property on Giles Street to be used for a school. The Cohansey Township School was built there in 1847, on the site of an earlier school.

In 1798, a society for "the promotion of Literature" was formed.[31] Subscribers paid seven dollars or more a year, and the result was the Harmony Academy, a school that occupied the lower floor of Brearley Lodge No. 9 on Bank Street. In 1846, Lodge No. 9 became Lodge No. 2. The Lodge occupied the upper floor of the building for its meeting rooms.

THE FIRST INDUSTRIES

Necessity brought the Industrial Revolution to Bridgetown. Due to Jefferson's Embargo Act and the War of 1812, there were very few imports into the United States from England and France from 1806 to 1815. Americans were forced to make their own goods. The East Lake Woolen Mill and the Cumberland Nail and Iron Works were among the most important industries in local history and certainly among the most lasting. Both began during the time of embargo, and both utilized Bridgetown's plentiful water supply.

Jeremiah Buck built three mills, which heralded the beginning of one economic era and the end of another. In 1807, he built a dam at East Lake and then a gristmill and a sawmill. In 1811, a woolen mill was constructed on East Commerce Street. It was the town's first heavy industry. During a storm in February 1822, the dam broke and the mill was destroyed. The owner at the time, Dr. William Elmer, rebuilt a bigger mill. The business became the East Lake Woolen Mill in 1866 after several name changes and owners. It employed 130 workers but went out of business when fire destroyed the building in 1902.

THE CUMBERLAND NAIL AND IRON WORKS

The Cumberland Nail and Iron Works opened in 1815 and dominated the economy for much of the nineteenth century. Like Bridgetown's earlier mills, it utilized the waterpower of the Cohansey River. Before Benjamin and David

Reeves of Camden opened the Nail Works, other would-be industrialists recognized the value of the Cohansey's natural power. In 1814, Ebenezer Seeley and James Lee proposed to build a paper mill to take advantage of the high price of paper during the War of 1812. The war ended, the price of paper dropped and the mill was not built, but the two had already altered the town's topography. They had joined efforts with Smith Bowen, who owned land on the west side of the river, and built a dam a mile north of town. Because the water flowed over a series of steps, the structure was known as Tumbling Dam. Sunset Lake was a byproduct of the endeavor. They also dug a raceway from the lake on the east side of the river to a sawmill near North Street.

The Reeves brothers bought Bowen's share of the dam's water power, and the Nail Works opened soon after. They built the raceway on the west side of the river to the site of their factory, at the present-day Morningside Park section of the city park.

Before the nail machine was invented, a blacksmith hammered out individual nails. Such nails were expensive and so valued that sometimes unused buildings were burned just to salvage the nails. The Reeves brothers took the original design for a nail machine, simplified it and then produced nails from scrap iron. By 1822, the sixteen machines of the Nail Works produced ten tons of high-quality nails each week. The nails sold for ten or fifteen cents a pound.

The company employed twenty-six men and boys at the time. Local churches provided night classes for boys who wanted to learn to read. The boy employees were usually at least twelve years old. They came from poor families, sometimes the families of adult millworkers. The youngsters were limited to simple tasks and running errands, but they worked twelve hours a day, six days a week, just like the adults.

Fire destroyed the buildings of the Nail Works in 1824. They were soon rebuilt. In 1843, a new method of cutting nails, along with the use of American iron, brought more change to the nail industry. By the 1860s, the price of nails had dropped to three and a half cents a pound. The number of employees at the Nail Works had increased to four hundred. More than one hundred machines produced 140,000 kegs of nails and four million feet of gas and water pipe each year.

The company built a rolling mill on the east side of the river in 1847, south of present-day Washington Street. In the rolling mill, pig iron was melted and rolled into sheets from which the nails were cut. Twenty furnaces and two trains of rollers fueled mill production there.

In 1853, a plant for manufacturing gas and water pipes was added. Reeves, Buck and Co., as the Nail Works was then called, maintained its

The Nail House was the office of the Cumberland Nail and Iron Works, which closed in 1899. It is now a museum. *Photo by Sam Feinstein.*

own Washington Street bridge between the rolling mill and the nail mill. Both mills were dirty, noisy and dangerous for the health of workers and surroundings. The plants dumped coal smoke into the air and ashes and other debris into the river, but that was common practice for nineteenth-century industry.

Industrial progress in the form of wire nails and steel pipes defeated the Nail Works. Cut nails could not compete with the new, cheap wire nails. Iron pipes, though longer-lasting, were no match for steel pipes made nearer to the sources of coal and iron. The Nail Works closed in 1899.

In 1903, the City of Bridgeton acquired the property for use as a public park. Today, the original office building of the Nail Works is maintained as a museum in the city park, with an old nail-cutting machine on display.

In the early nineteenth century, Bridgetown was a very small town, but it was growing fast and prospering. The population increased dramatically, from 400 residents in 1814 to 1,736 in 1829. The woolen mill and Nail Works were new but expanding businesses. Glassmaking was an important industry from its beginning in the 1830s. The major industries in the county were agriculture and lumbering. Twenty-five vessels left Bridgetown wharves to deliver twenty-eight thousand cords of wood each year, all cut from the cedar and pine forests ringing the town. Visualize a wall of wood four feet wide, four feet high and over forty-two miles long. All that wood was fuel, first for the fireplaces and then later for the stoves of Philadelphia. Colonel David Potter was reputed to own sixty teams of mules, which transported lumber and grain to his fleet of schooners.

THE FIRST BANK

On October 23, 1815, the *Washington Whig*, a weekly newspaper, published the following notice: "The citizens of Bridgetown friendly to the establishment of a BANK are requested to meet at the Court House tomorrow evening; the 24th inst., at 7 o'clock."

The editor, Peter Hay, never reported the outcome of the meeting, but a week later, he expressed skepticism that both Bridgetown and Port Elizabeth would be granted permission by the state legislature to establish banks. Later, as the bank came nearer to reality, Editor Hay predicted it would fail. He was wrong; almost two hundred years later, the bank is still in business, though it has changed its name several times.

The legislature approved an "Act to establish the Cumberland Bank in the town of Bridgeton in the County of Cumberland" on February 15, 1816. This was the first time the growing town was called Bridgeton rather than Bridgetown. This disproves the charming legend that the "w" disappeared from "Bridgetown" because a printer who was working on stationery for the new bank dropped it. In 1816, Rahway in North Jersey was called Bridgetown, too. The name change was probably made in Trenton to avoid confusion between Bridgetown East and Bridgetown West in the conduct of state business. The name of the port remained Bridgetown, however.

The establishment of the bank solidified Bridgetown/Bridgeton as the financial center of the county. The bank sold stocks at $50 a share, with the full amount payable in forty years. The majority of the 168 stockholders owned fewer than twenty shares. In 1816, $500 represented the annual earnings of a bank clerk. Therefore, the purchase of ten shares was far beyond the means of an average family. Some of the major stockholders included Jeremiah Buck, sixty shares; the Reeves brothers, twenty shares each; and James Giles of Bridgeton, forty shares. Benjamin Cooper of Camden was the largest stockholder with one hundred shares.

Within sixty days, Jeremiah Buck built the bank at Bridge Street at the foot of Freemason Street. The original building now forms part of the Bridgeton Library. The streets are now called Commerce and Bank Streets.

Dr. Jonathan Elmer served as bank president for just a month. General James Giles succeeded him and was president until his death in 1825. In the beginning, the bank served Salem, Cape May and Cumberland Counties and parts of Gloucester County. It had no competition until a Millville bank opened in 1857.

When William G. Nixon became the president of the Cumberland National Bank in 1886, the Davis Hotel was demolished to make way for a new bank

A drawing of the original Cumberland Bank building of 1816. The building is an integral part of the Bridgeton Free Public Library. *Conjectural sketch by Penelope Watson.*

building. The hotel had been the elegant home of John Moore White. The new building opened for business in May 1887. William G. Nixon III, who conducted research for the original edition of this history, offered a family view of his great-grandfather. The earlier Nixon, while possessing a very real financial talent, may have ensured his advancement from clerk to cashier, and eventually to bank president, by the method often used by the heroes of the Horatio Alger books. Those young men rose from rags to riches through hard work and pluck and with the help of a wealthy patron. Nixon's wife, Sarah, was the daughter of James Boyd Potter, president of the bank. It took Nixon forty-seven years to achieve his goal, but there was financial reward along the way. The cashier of the Cumberland Bank earned twice as much as the president at the time. Nixon was sixty-eight when he became chief officer of the bank. He held that position until 1907, when he died at age eighty-nine.

MAIL AND SHIPPING

Daily mail service began in 1816 too. Perhaps it was brought on by the needs of the bank and Nail Works and other industries. In addition, daily stagecoach routes were available to take passengers to Philadelphia via

Salem or Woodbury. A steamboat completed the journey from Salem, and a train covered the final leg between Woodbury and Philadelphia. Every morning except Sunday, a four-horse stage left the Davis Hotel at 8:00 a.m. for the journey to Salem and Philadelphia. Fare for the eight-hour excursion was $1.50.

After the U.S. Constitution was adopted in 1787, Congress designated Bridgetown as the official port of entry for the southern part of New Jersey for foreign commerce as well as coastal trade. The port was called Bridgetown until the 1870s, long after the town had changed its name to Bridgeton. The first collector of the port was Colonel Eli Elmer. The shipping trade that flourished on the Cohansey River contributed to Bridgeton's growth as well. The United States Senate appointed General Ebenezer Elmer the collector of the Port of Bridgetown in 1822.

Ship arrivals and departures were reported in the *Washington Whig*. Shipbuilding was an important activity along the Cohansey at Bridgeton, Fairton and Port Norris. Schooners and sloops were built for bay and coastal trade. They would first sail on the Cohansey River, so they could not be too large. Bridgeton shipbuilding continued until the 1930s. The *Washington Whig* reported a typical launching:

> *On Tuesday last, April 19, 1825, the fine sloop,* General Jackson, *between 60 and 70 tons burthen, owned by Jeremiah Stull, Esq., of Salem County, and Richard Hann of Bridgeton, was launched into the Cohansey, from the shipyard adjoining the Free Landing in this town, superbly painted and decked with beauteous streamers flying. After the launch an excellent dinner was given by the owners at the Lafayette Hotel, kept by Mr. John Hann Jr.*

THE FIRST SUCCESSFUL NEWSPAPER

The *Washington Whig* was Bridgeton's first successful newspaper, owned by Peter Hay and published for the first time on July 24, 1815. In 1837, James M. Newell, publisher of the *West Jersey Observer*, bought the *Washington Whig* and combined the two papers into one, the *Bridgeton Chronicle*.

Newspaper advertisements were often poignant, such as this one: "That my wife has left my bed and board and I will not be responsible for any bills incurred by her." Names of husband and wife accompanied such notices. More mundane notices proclaimed the virtues of various hats, houses, horses and clothing or sought the whereabouts of runaway child employees.

The Nail Works was not the only employer of children. Throughout this era, it was common for families to place their children with craftsmen to learn a trade or with wealthy families to assist in household work. If assigned to a craftsman, a boy was called an apprentice. If a child was taken into a home, he or she was called "bound." Children were often unhappy with such arrangements, and the *Whig* printed notices like the following almost daily: "July 26, 1834—SIX CENTS REWARD—Ran away from the subscriber, on the 11th inst. An indented apprentice boy to the Blacksmith Business, named William Harris, about five feet high, dark complection, dark hair and eyes. Had on dark everyday clothes. Joseph Gibson, Bridgeton."

"February 7, 1820—For Sale—The time of a smart active Negro Girl, between 10 and 11 years old, has about 11 years to serve. Inquire of Robert Seeley, in Bridgeton."

THE COUNTY SEAT CONTESTED

Much of the early growth and development of Bridgeton was connected to its position as county seat and the related activities: courts, board of chosen freeholders, county clerk's and surrogate's offices, sheriff's office and the jail. Around 1832, the courthouse, which stood inconveniently in the middle of Broad Street, was deemed too small and in need of replacement. In 1836, the freeholders bought a property at the corner of Fayette and Broad Streets with plans to construct the new courthouse there.

However, the population of the eastern part of the county had grown, and residents of Millville and Fairfield Township lobbied to change the county seat to their locales. Some contended that Fairfield Township would have been the original county seat but was hampered by an entanglement of land title disputes. The freeholders decided to take no action until county landowners could indicate their preference in an election. Bridgeton won, but the freeholders were not required by law to heed the results of the election, and it was rumored that the Millville and Fairfield supporters would join forces just for spite.

Bridgeton supporters then claimed that the old courthouse was good enough and times were too hard to spend money for a new, larger building. For the next several years, the question of the building was proposed at almost every meeting of the freeholders, with four voting for the building (which almost guaranteed Millville as the new county seat) and four against. The stalemate continued for six years, with the two Bridgeton newspapers

The courthouse, jail and sheriff's house, 1876. Note the jail at center back right, with bars on the windows. *Drawing from 1876* Historic Atlas of Cumberland County, *courtesy of Karen Horwitz.*

taking opposite sides. The overseer of roads did his part when he served the board with notice that the present courthouse was illegally blocking Broad Street and the freeholders would have to move it.

The lively issue ensured perfect attendance at every meeting of the freeholders, regardless of weather, health or other commitments. If anyone missed a meeting, the tie vote would be broken, and the opposite view would prevail.

An unknown, enterprising politico found a way out of the impasse. In March 1844, a new township called Columbia was created out of parts of Hopewell and Stow Creek Townships, with the village of Shiloh in the center of it. The new township supported a Bridgeton courthouse. The tie was broken, the new majority prevailed and the freeholders of the four eastern townships capitulated gracefully to cooperate with the construction of the new courthouse. The following year, Columbia Township was dissolved. Today, all that remains of Columbia is a crossroad north of Shiloh known as Columbia Corners. A road from that point leading to Seeley is known as Columbia Highway. When the first edition of this history was written, a few Millville residents still maintained that had there not been political hanky-panky on the part of the Bridgetonians, today the county seat would be located in Millville. They reasoned that it was a matter of fairness and justice since Millville is closer to the geographic center of the county than Bridgeton.

The new courthouse was built at the corner of Fayette and Broad Streets and completed before the end of 1844. Bridgeton's original Liberty Bell was removed from the belfry of the old courthouse and given to West Jersey Academy in 1852. The Cumberland County Historical Society owns it now.

The courthouse cost $10,674.43, including fencing, landscaping, furniture and fixtures. The old brick courthouse, which had blocked the east end of Broad Street for eighty-four years, was sold for $85.00 and soon torn down. The steep hill behind it was graded down to the river. The entrance to Potter's Tavern, which had been at street level, was then elevated eight feet above the sloping roadway, as it remains. Broad Street was still a dusty, unpaved road traveled by carriages, wagons and riders on horseback. The street was sprinkled with water each day to calm the noxious dust raised by all the traffic.

TWIN TOWNS ON THE COHANSEY

Even after Cohansey Bridge became the county seat in 1747/8, it was not really a town. Residents simply regarded it as the area around the bridge. The courthouse was located in Hopewell Township, and the area east of the bridge was in Deerfield Township. There is no evidence of a common civic interest, shared community pride or even awareness that events that took place on one side of the river affected the other side. This could have been a product of early property practices. Land surveys always stopped at the edge of a body of water and did not continue to the other side. Whatever the cause, for early residents, the county seat was separated from the life of the community. It was a District of Columbia in miniature.

Public sentiment did not change, despite the changes in name. First the area was Cohansey Bridge or the Bridge, then Bridgetown in 1765 and finally Bridgeton in 1816. However, when the census of 1830 showed the combined population of Hopewell and Deerfield was 2,044, some progressive townspeople wanted to petition the legislature to combine the settlements on both sides of the river into one township.

Residents who lived on the east side of the river withdrew from Deerfield Township and formed Bridgeton Township. Three years later, their neighbors across the river withdrew from Hopewell and established

Cohansey Township. They resisted consolidation with Bridgeton for twenty years. The townships of Bridgeton and Cohansey were incorporated as the city of Bridgeton in March 1865, with a mayor-council form of government.

THE HEALTH OF THE PEOPLE

Everyday life affronted the health of eighteenth- and nineteenth-century residents. The ever-present road dust irritated their throats, lungs and eyes. Some diary writers of the period regarded the air itself as an unhealthy force. In 1774, Philip Vickers Fithian, living in Greenwich, wrote of "wet weather, fluxes and horse distempers."[32] A year later, he wrote:

> *News from below that many disorders, chiefly the flux, are now raging in the lower counties, Chester, etc. I pray God Delaware may be a bar, and stop that painful and deadly disorder. Enough has it ravaged our poor Cohansians. Enough are we in Cohansey every autumn enfeebled and wasted with the ague and fever. Our children all grow pale, puny and lifeless.*[33]

Ague and bloody flux were malaria and the dysentery that often accompanies it. At the time, doctors did not know that the anopheles mosquito carried the disease. In tropical countries, Peruvian bark (quinine) was used to treat malaria. In his journal entry for October 18, 1773, Fithian describes taking Peruvian bark for the first time. But he had referred to his own "fits" of chills and fever as early as 1766. He wrote that these bouts interrupted his work on the family farm.

The horse distemper of Fithian's account was equine encephalitis, another disease transmitted by mosquitoes. Mosquitoes continued to thrive along the Cohansey, but the dangerous varieties disappeared in the 1820s. L.Q.C. Elmer's history of Cumberland County offered one explanation:

> *After the enlargement of the mill pond east of Bridgeton in 1809, and the raising of the new pond northward in 1814, intermittent and bilious fevers were common in Bridgeton for successive years. In 1823 these diseases prevailed to a fearful extent; but after this, in the course of three or four years they ceased to prevail either in the town or other parts of the county. The improvement has been ascribed to more perfect draining, and to the use of lime for agricultural purposes. But while it is probable that these causes had some effect, the change was too sudden, and has been too great to be*

ascribed mainly to them. Atmospheric, telluric (proceeding from the earth),
or other influences far more potent, must have occurred.[34]

Despite the author's wish for a more mystical cause, the use of lime on outhouses and fields was probably the miracle cure.

Typhoid caused many deaths, too. Given the congestion of the growing population and the accepted sanitary practices, conditions were ideal for typhoid fever. Behind every house was a shallow open well, located where it could be reached by the effluent from the family privy. Likewise, waste from the barn, which housed horses and cows, or even the pigsty, which served as a garbage disposal unit, could flow into a family's water supply. Considering these arrangements, it is not surprising that many people contracted what was described as a "malignant, nondescript fever." It is surprising that anyone avoided the malady. From 1815 to 1817, six Cumberland County doctors, working until they were exhausted, were infected by contact with patients and died.

Ephraim Harris, a resident of Fairfield, kept a journal of his experiences as a soldier during the Revolutionary War. He also described a smallpox epidemic: "That fatal and never to be forgotten year of 1759 when the Lord sent the destroying angel to pass through this place, and removed many of our friends into eternity in a short space of time; not a house exempt, not a family spared from the calamity. So dreadful was it that it made every ear tingle, and every heart bleed."[35]

People simply did not take the appropriate measures to protect themselves from disease. For example, during the summer months, window screens were an unknown refinement. Open doors and windows attracted myriad flies, which bred on the countless manure heaps in the town. Mosquitoes from nearby swamps and meadows and other buzzing, biting insects were unwelcome guests. Smudge fires were built outside homes to repel gnats and mosquitoes during early evening hours so a family could rest. Even after cotton netting from India was introduced as screening, some diehards resisted its use. It was somehow a display of un-American weakness to admit to an inability to endure the presence of a few mosquitoes or flies in the house. As late as the 1880s, a Bridgeton homeowner vetoed the use of window screens in his newly constructed house. He did not want any "strained air."[36]

With the introduction of lime and a general improvement in sanitary practices, ague and the bloody flux were eliminated. At the end of the nineteenth century, one writer could boast of the pleasant climate and the good health and low death rate of Bridgeton's inhabitants.[37]

GENERAL JAMES GILES AND HIS HOUSE

Because his mansion on Broad Street has been preserved, the name of General James Giles is a familiar one to many Bridgetonians. His illustrious contemporaries—Dr. Jonathan Elmer, General Ebenezer Elmer, Colonel David Potter and Judge L.Q.C. Elmer—no doubt surpassed Giles in accomplishments. But their homes no longer exist, and their names, therefore, are known primarily to historians.

Giles was born in New York in 1759, the son of an Episcopalian clergyman. Soon after the Revolution began, and when he was not yet twenty years old, he was made a lieutenant in the New York Artillery under General Lafayette's command. It may be during his association with Lafayette that General Giles acquired a taste for elegant living, as demonstrated during his life in Bridgeton. Giles continued in military service until 1782. Tradition maintains he was an intimate of George Washington, but no proof exists.

In civilian life, Giles studied law in Trenton under Joseph Bloomfield. After being licensed in 1783, he married Bloomfield's sister. That same year, Bloomfield became attorney general of New Jersey. Giles practiced law in New York for a few years and then, perhaps on the advice of Bloomfield, moved to Bridgetown in 1788. He soon established a lucrative law practice and served as clerk of Cumberland County from 1789 to 1804. Giles became a general in the New Jersey Militia upon promotion by his brother-in-law who was then governor of New Jersey.

Giles was known as "a well-read lawyer and safe counselor; but it cannot be said that he was distinguished as an advocate. He was a small man, precise in his dress and in all he did. At the circuits he was one of the most genial and delightful companions. His legal documents were marked with great exactness and precision."[38]

In New York, Giles had been secretary of a Grand Lodge of Masons, and he helped form Brearley Lodge No. 9 in Bridgetown. In 1790, he became first high priest of that chapter.

When the Cumberland Bank was organized in 1816, General Giles was one of the five major stockholders. On September 9, 1816, he became president of the bank, a position he held until his death in 1825. He enjoyed living and traveling in luxury. He used an open carriage accompanied by a driver and footman. It was the nineteenth-century equivalent of a chauffeur-driven Rolls-Royce.

The Giles home, built in 1791, featured a formal garden, with the icehouse decorated with a wooden statue carved by William Rush, the first native-born

The General Giles House. This building is listed on the National Register of Historic Places. The Georgian house was built in 1791. *Photo by Sam Feinstein.*

American sculptor. The statue was a gift from Eli Elmer, collector of the Port of Bridgetown, the town's first postmaster and a neighbor of Giles. The statue had been the figurehead on *Ship John*, which sank in the Delaware Bay in 1797. The statue is now on display, courtesy of the Cumberland County Historical Society. The icehouse was really a deep cellar dug in the family garden and covered with a mound of earth. A gazebo or statue was often added to give an elegant note to this nicety of late eighteenth-century life.

The General Giles house is considered an outstanding example of post-Colonial architecture. It is listed on the National Register of Historic Places and is privately owned now.

THE COMMERCE STREET BRIDGE, REPAIRS AND REPLACEMENTS

Only the most essential repairs were made to the original Cohansey bridge until John Moore White claimed his inheritance. White wanted to build wharves north of the old bridge, and he needed a drawbridge to fulfill his plan. He donated land for a public landing and offered to pay for part of

The Commerce Street Bridge was damaged by the flood of 1934, the worst flood in the city's history. The three city bridges were all destroyed, and a pontoon bridge was put up so people could cross the river. *Courtesy of Jim Bergmann.*

the bridge and its upkeep. The county accepted his offer because the lumber industry was the main industry at the time and Philadelphia was the most important market for lumber. A drawbridge would help the lumber trade and ease the way for Philadelphia-bound vessels.

But then, as now, the location of any important public facility, like a bridge, was often the center of controversy. A group, led by George Burgin, builder of the stone storehouse at the corner of Broad and Atlantic Streets, wanted the new bridge built on Broad Street. In 1799, the board of freeholders agreed to build a new bridge (more than twenty-one feet wide) on Commerce Street. They built the bridge two years later, and White paid his promised share. The county expense was $3,000.

In February 1822, a flash flood destroyed every dam in the county. Floodwaters from Bostwick Lake, Seeley Lake, Hand's Pond and Silver Lake poured into Sunset Lake and the surrounding area. The flood severely damaged the Commerce Street Bridge. In 1833, that bridge was replaced by a twenty-six-foot-wide drawbridge, which was built by David Reeves of the Cumberland Nail Works for the county for $4,000. The coal used to fuel the rolling mill arrived on steamboats, and the finished nails went out on steamboats. A wide bridge was an asset to the Nail Works. That bridge functioned for about sixteen years and was then almost completely refurbished. Only the old abutments remained.

In 1875, the board of freeholders built the fifth Commerce Street span, a pivot bridge of stone and wrought iron. The flood of August 3, 1934, heralded the end of this bridge when a runaway oyster schooner crashed into it. The long-awaited Broad Street Bridge was built in 1869.

EARLY STREETS

With the construction of the first bridge, Main or Bridge Street became an important Bridgeton and county thoroughfare. It was later known as Commerce Street. In 1775, the street extended from the bridge to Seeley's Millpond/East Lake. By 1801, it extended to Burlington Road and to Millville. In 1853, the turnpike to Millville became a toll road.

Broad Street, previously Main or High Street, is the oldest street in Bridgeton. The Concessions and Agreements of 1676 required the construction of a street one hundred feet wide. The presence of the courthouse and jail from the earliest days of the town ensured the street's importance.

Vine Street was one of the original streets, but the date of its beginning is unknown. In 1796, it was laid out four rods (sixty-six feet) wide.

Originally, Fayette Street was a trail that connected Broad Street to a Dutch and Swedish settlement in Dutch Neck. In 1796, that roadway was also widened to four rods and its course altered, from Broad Street to Cubby's Hollow.

Laurel Street began as a short road from Commerce Street to Hance Woolson's wharf, where the Broad Street Bridge now crosses the river. Laurel Street was extended in both directions until it met Loper's Run at the north and Glass Street at the south.

CHAPTER 5

A VICTORIAN BOOMTOWN

In 1750, Cohansey Bridge was a primitive settlement with no more than 75 inhabitants. By 1850, the population had grown to almost 3,500 residents living in 670 dwellings. Most of the town's business was conducted on Commerce Street. Homes clustered on East and West Commerce, Cohansey, Laurel, Pearl, Bank, Pine, Water, Atlantic, Broad, Fayette and Franklin Streets. Two neighborhoods reflected growing industries. The houses ringing the grist- and woolen mills on East Commerce Street made up Milltown.

The Shops at Cohansey Crossing, built in the mid-nineteenth century, are still used by retail businesses. It is the oldest commercial block in the city. *Drawing by Karen Horwitz.*

Glasstown was the area surrounding the glassworks on South Pearl Street. Laurel Hill on North Laurel Street was another growing neighborhood.

Most roads were dirt roads, except for Commerce Street, which had been filled with an eight- to ten-inch layer of oyster shells.[39] The few real sidewalks were made of brick. Trees lined Bridgeton streets, but lampposts did not. Bridgeton had no lights after dark. People and vehicles crossed the Cohansey over the wooden Commerce Street Bridge. The major industries were the same ones that had dominated the economy at the beginning of the century: the Cumberland Nail and Iron Works, the Cohansey Glass Works (earlier Stratton and Buck) and the East Lake Woolen Mill.

The system of public education had improved somewhat. In 1847, the town erected a school on Bank Street, and the following year, the Cohansey School was built on the corner of Giles and Academy Streets. Bridgeton had grown since the early days of the century, but life had not changed much. Important changes came during and after the Civil War.

THE CIVIL WAR AND THE CUMBERLAND GREYS

Fort Sumter, South Carolina, fell on April 14, 1861. On April 20, Congressman John T. Nixon presided over a Bridgeton rally featuring patriotic speeches and resolutions. On April 23, Sheppard's Hall on Commerce Street became a recruiting station. Within two days, 101 men had enlisted for the Union cause. This company was affectionately known as the Cumberland Greys, officially Company F, Third Regiment, New Jersey Infantry. Its members formed the first group of volunteers from the county. They were called the Greys because as militia members, they wore grey uniforms. When they became part of the Union force, they donned Union blue. Captain James W. Stickney, First Lieutenant Samuel T. DuBois and Second Lieutenant George Woodruff led Company F.

On May 27, 1861, the Cumberland Greys departed from the Bridgeton Wharf on the steamer *Patuxent*, bound for Philadelphia. Business was suspended for the day, and the whole community gathered to see the recruits off.[40] The Greys participated in forty-three engagements, beginning with the first Battle of Bull Run and ending with the surrender at Appomattox. Seventeen of the Greys died in battle or from wounds or illness aggravated by battle conditions.

A notable Bridgeton recruit was Sergeant Bowman H. Buck, known as "Old Chapultepec." He had served with General Winfield Scott's army in the Mexican War, at the attack on the fortress Chapultepec. During the Civil War, he was present at the Battles of Bull Run, Malvern Hill, Fredericksburg, Chancellorsville, Antietam, Gettysburg, Spotsylvania, the Wilderness, Petersburg and Richmond. He emerged from all that action without injury and reenlisted in time to be present at Appomattox for Lee's surrender.[41]

The fervor of Bridgeton's military allegiance was expressed at home, too. When townsfolk questioned the loyalties of a popular minister, he was forced to resign his post. The Reverend Samuel Beach Jones had been a much-loved and able pastor for the First Presbyterian Church, then on Laurel Street. When members of his congregation and others outside his church suspected him of being a Southern sympathizer, he resigned. His brother, Paul T. Jones, on the other hand, was a leading Northern supporter who delivered a rousing speech during the farewell ceremony for the Cumberland Greys.

In 1862, Bridgeton men answered another call for recruits and joined Company K, Twelfth Regiment, New Jersey Infantry. They left on a train from the railroad station on Irving Avenue on August 12.[42] Company K soldiers fought at Chancellorsville, Gettysburg and other battles and observed Lee's surrender. Twenty-three of them died, some of them at the infamous prison camp at Andersonville, Georgia.

Less than a month after Company K departed, 300 more men enlisted at the Bridgeton recruiting office. This time they joined the Twenty-fourth New Jersey Regiment. In 1863, Bridgeton volunteers signed up to join Company H, Third Regiment, New Jersey Cavalry. Some of the 117 men of the company had completed their service with the Cumberland Greys and reenlisted. Company H reported twelve deaths among its ranks. Between the massive recruiting drives, individuals joined other units, but the companies described here were basically Bridgeton units.

During one recruiting drive, more than three hundred men enlisted in three days. "This patriotic feat was never exceeded in any part of the nation during the war, and had but one parallel—that of the town of Haverhill, Massachusetts, where about the same number were enlisted at the same time."[43] Although Bridgeton's support of the Union was heroic and outstanding, the praise is misleading. The enlistment office was in Bridgeton, but volunteers came from other parts of the county as well as Bridgeton. Later, when a draft was imposed, unwilling draftees were permitted to pay substitutes to take their places. Support for the war was not unanimous in Bridgeton or anywhere else. Draft avoidance was tolerated by official policy.

The civilian population devoured war news as eagerly as soldiers did. Northern victories at Gettysburg and Vicksburg caused much jubilation in

Bridgeton. The town rang its church bells and fire bells. Local bands, both organized and impromptu, played out of joy and relief. Everybody sang patriotic songs, and some people drank toasts at local taverns. When the war was over, the celebration was short-lived. President Lincoln was dead, and joy was tempered with grief. Bridgeton's heroes returned more quietly than they had left. The war had dragged on for four years, much longer than anybody had anticipated.

POSTWAR BOOM

In 1865, Bridgeton was incorporated as a city, bringing the townships of Bridgeton and Cohansey together with a mayor-council form of government. James Hood was the first mayor. City Council, called Common Council in those days, first met on April 17, three days after the assassination of Abraham Lincoln. The first order of business was recognition of that sad event:

> *Whereas, Abraham Lincoln President of the United States was on the evening of Friday last, in the City of Washington most foully murdered by the hand of an assassin.*
>
> *And whereas In his death the American people have lost a Patriotic & able President & the cause of the Union & of Humanity & of Liberty its most devoted champion.*
>
> *And whereas the Mayor & Common Council of the City of Bridgeton at their first meeting desire to put upon record their profound sense of personal & Public Loss in this Sad national calamity. Therefore*
>
> *1st Be it resolved that in the death of Abraham Lincoln the people of the United States North & South have lost their best friend & benefactor. That whilst the hand of the assassin held the instrument it was Treason & Slavery which directed the Shot that extinguished his illustrious Life, and that whilst we desire to Submit without a murmur to the dispensations of an overruling Providence we pledge anew over his grave our fealty to our Country and to the great cause of popular right to which he dies the victim.*

Bridgeton's participation in the war had been generous and patriotic. The town's postwar activity was equally vigorous. "By 1880 Bridgeton was the largest city in the state south of Camden, with a population of almost nine thousand. It was the leading manufacturing town in South Jersey."[44] By

The corner of Laurel and Commerce Streets shows the hustle and bustle at the center of town in the early 1900s during Bridgeton's golden age. *Courtesy of Jim Bergmann.*

1890, the number of houses had risen to 3,000, more than double the 1870 total of 1,325.

Bridgeton was poised for its golden age. New shipyards, canning factories, glass factories and retail stores appeared. Increased means of transportation reflected the town's growth. Stagecoaches and boats continued their routes until 1875 and later. By then, three railroads carried passengers and freight through town. In July 1861, the West Jersey Railroad completed a line from Woodbury with the Bridgeton depot at Bank Street and Irving Avenue. In the 1890s, the depot moved to the corner of Lemon and South Pearl Streets. That location is now West Broad and South Pearl, and the depot was for a time the home of the Bridgeton-Cumberland Tourist Association. That railroad route became part of the Pennsylvania-Reading Seashore Lines.

In 1872, the New Jersey Southern Railroad finished the line from Bay Side on the Delaware River to Vineland, via Bridgeton and Greenwich, and north to Jersey City. This was a revolutionary change that opened northern markets for the area. Eventually, the line merged with the New Jersey Central Railroad.

The Bridgeton–Port Norris Railroad was completed in 1875 and almost immediately reorganized as the Cumberland and Maurice River Railroad. Its principal cargo was oysters, eight to fifteen carloads a day. As the glass industry developed, however, sand replaced oysters as the most important product shipped by the railroad. This line also merged with the New Jersey Central Railroad.

The trains arrived daily, carrying passengers and freight to a community bursting with prosperity. The dominant industries of the early nineteenth century—the Nail Works, the Cohansey Glass Works and the East Lake Woolen Mill—maintained their importance. They were joined and eventually overshadowed by a host of other factories.

OBERLIN SMITH

Factories and businesses multiplied. One of the most important new factories, the Ferracute Machine Co., began as Smith and Webb in 1863. Ferracute's founder, Oberlin Smith, was a contemporary of Henry Ford and Thomas Edison. Local folklore has placed Smith in the company and friendship of the others. Smith had business dealings with Ford and some correspondence with Edison, but he was not a member of their social circle. Smith's inventions were important in press manufacturing, and his contributions to engineering and machine building stand on their own. His accomplishments were valuable and not dependent on friendships with famous men.

He was elected president of the American Society of Mechanical Engineers in 1889. He was called "one of the most accomplished draughtsmen and skilful [sic] inventors of the day."[45] Smith invented magnetic recording. Without it, there would be no audio or video recording or computer disk drives. He held over seventy patents for his inventions and received the last one just weeks before he died at age eighty-six. He developed his first invention when he was a teenage employee of the Nail Works. He was known for giving delightful parties and for being an excellent dancer. Oberlin Smith was, most definitely, a Renaissance man for his time, or any time.

Smith was an enlightened employer who required employees to pursue additional education and then rewarded them when they did. He built his company into a press-building firm known throughout the world. For example, the government of China sought Ferracute knowhow and bought Ferracute coin presses for the minting of its coins. Ferracute exhibited its products at the major business expositions so popular in the United States and Europe in the late 1800s and early 1900s. Yet Smith chose to stay in Bridgeton, maintaining both home and factory there, to the benefit of the local economy and individual employees.[46]

Left: Oberlin Smith is pictured in his formal portrait as the ninth president of the American Society of Mechanical Engineers (1890–91). *Courtesy of Arthur Cox.*

Below: The interior of Oberlin Smith's Ferracute Machine Co., circa 1915, demonstrates Smith's concept of a congenial workplace. *Courtesy of Arthur Cox.*

The Ferracute Company and other machine shops developed from the inventive skill of unusual individuals. The Hettinger Machine Works, for example, began in 1898 and specialized in gasoline engines. Hettinger built the first gas engine in Bridgeton and gas marine engines used in the eastern and southern United States.

GLASSWORKS

Ferracute made products for specialized markets. Other industries of the period relied on general supply and demand. The glass industry was such an enterprise. Glass was Bridgeton's most important product for over a century. One of Cumberland County's abundant resources is a type of sand ideal for glassmaking. So Bridgeton was a natural glassmaking center, with its excellent railroad facilities and supply of water, lumber and sand. Factories in Millville and Vineland also produced glass. Glassmaking remains important in Bridgeton even today with Leone Industries. Bridgeton's first glass factory, Stratton and Buck Co., was established in 1836.

In 1889, Bridgeton supported twenty glass factories, which turned out window glass, bottles of all sizes and colors, canning jars and industrial and laboratory glass containers. Nineteenth-century glassmaking required skilled workers because all the glass was hand blown. The talents and sensibility of such highly skilled and well-paid workers contributed to the general prosperity.

In the 1880s, Bridgeton's oldest and largest glass factory was the Cohansey Glass Works, which had its roots in Stratton and Buck Co. It had a peak time workforce of five hundred men and boys. Its three window glass and three bottle (hollow ware) plants covered a five-acre plot on South Pearl, Glass and Mill Streets. The Cohansey fruit jar was a patented design of the Cohansey Glass Works.

The Cumberland Glass Company later surpassed the Cohansey firm in size and importance, however. Cumberland Glass began as Joseph A. Clark and Co. and was organized in 1880 at a plant on Water Street but soon moved to larger quarters on North Laurel Street. The company later bought the More, Jonas, More plant on Bank Street. In its early days, the company employed three hundred men and boys who produced a great variety of glass items.

After World War I, the Illinois Glass Company bought Cumberland Glass and then merged with the Owens Glass Company of Toledo, Ohio, to become the Owens-Illinois Glass Company, Bridgeton's largest factory and the backbone of its twentieth century economy.

This Lewis Wickes Hine photograph shows a midnight scene in the More-Jonas Glass Works in Bridgeton in 1909. Some of the workers are quite young, in particular the "snapper-up boy" at left. *Library of Congress collection.*

Other glass companies were Clark Window Glass; the Getsinger Glass Works; the West Side Glass Manufacturing Co.; More, Jonas, More; and East Lake Glass Works. The Cumberland Nail and Iron Works continued to make its products during this period, too. Many of these companies boasted of the loyalty of their employees, who worked decades, often for their entire productive lives. They started as apprentices, often in boyhood, and continued with the same employer for years.

AGRICULTURE

Agriculture was one of the county's most important industries, and tomatoes, beans, peaches, apples and berries were the most important exports. Bridgeton canning plants processed the local crops. In 1860, Stein Edwards established the first of Bridgeton's six nineteenth-century canneries. By 1888, it was incorporated as the West Jersey Packing Company. It produced its own cans and packed Jersey tomatoes, peaches, lima beans, sweet potatoes, catsup and salad dressing. West Jersey employed 175 men and women during the busy season.

Tomato wagons waiting to be unloaded at the canning factory on Water Street. *Courtesy of Karen Horwitz.*

The John W. Stout Cannery, at the corner of Bank Street and Irving Avenue, appeared in the 1860s. It, too, made its own cans and employed 175 men and women. Stout's Cannery was known for its "Red X" brand fruits and vegetables. Cumberland County Packing and Canning Co., Probasco and Laning, B.S. Ayers and J.F. Brady and Co. were the other canners. Each factory employed from 140 to 200 workers during the season.

Local farming was important to the canneries. Boyd's Directory for 1881–82 lists 270 Bridgeton farmers, some of whom maintained small farms within city limits. Others worked on farms outside of town.

Other Bridgeton factories produced cloth, paper, leather, lumber and metal goods, shoes, flour, carriages and pottery. Cox and Sons made steam-heating equipment, steam engines and boilers. The Perfection Funnel Works turned out tin, copper and glass funnels in all the standard sizes. The plant employed twenty men and boys. In 1886, the Lucknow Paper Mill at the foot of Hampton Street produced rag paper in white and colors. In 1887, Lott's Flour Mill, located at the corner of Commerce Street and the park entrance, ground seventy-five barrels of flour each day.

This map shows the serpentine course of the Cohansey River, which meanders for twenty-three miles from the Delaware Bay to Bridgeton. *From 1876* Historical Atlas of Cumberland County, *courtesy of Karen Horwitz.*

THE PORT OF BRIDGETON

Shipping and shipbuilding thrived throughout the nineteenth century. Bridgeton was part of a coastal shipping network that existed along the eastern seaboard. As South Jersey's premier manufacturing center, Bridgeton was a logical goal for ships. But sailors must have viewed the Cohansey River as a challenge. As the crow flies, the distance from the Delaware Bay to Bridgeton is seven miles. But the river meanders a serpentine course from its mouth to Bridgeton, twenty-three miles away. Generally, the river flows south from Bridgeton to Fairton, west to Greenwich and south to the bay. Despite the wayward river, however, boats were a popular means of transport.

Bridgeton shipyards built coastal and seagoing vessels. John Pugh (Pew) built Bridgeton's first steam vessel in 1854. Joseph Bitting and Enos Ayars built ships during the 1850s. Bridgeton shipyards built more than 150 schooners and sloops, many of them seaworthy, from 1846 to 1901. Lehman Blew and William Rice owned important shipyards on the east bank of the river.

Bridgeton remained a port of entry, with its custom house in the post office building on East Commerce Street. The building now serves as the city hall annex. Over five hundred ships, mainly coastal vessels or oyster boats, were registered at the Bridgeton port during its busy years.

Commercial transport shifted to the railroads after the Civil War. The journey over water from Bridgeton to Camden or Philadelphia consumed a whole day. A stagecoach ride took six hours, but the train trip to Camden/Philadelphia was less than three hours long. Goods ordered from Philadelphia were often delivered over water when speed was not a necessity. But attempts to run passenger boats from Bridgeton to Philadelphia always failed because boats could not beat trains for speed.

Shipping was but one aspect of Bridgeton's prosperity. The town was a lively retail center as well and promoted its "large, well-stocked and well-conducted business marts."[47] W.W. Robbins on North Laurel Street was the largest of five clothing stores. Six merchants dealt in dry goods. The business community had thirty-six grocers, fourteen dressmakers, three billiard parlors, four bakers, eight druggists, eight lawyers or law firms, eighteen physicians, three hotels, four variety stores, five saloons (including one lager beer saloon), three furniture dealers, five justices of the peace, two piano stores and four harness makers.[48]

NEWSPAPERS AND POLITICS

Six newspapers vied for readers in the 1880s and 1890s. The weeklies were the *Bridgeton Pioneer*, the *New Jersey Patriot*, the *Bridgeton Chronicle* and *Dollar Weekly News*. The *Bridgeton Evening News* and *Daily Pioneer* appeared daily.[49] Newspapers did not hide their political bias. The *Pioneer* was known as the leading Republican newspaper of the county.[50] The *Bridgeton Chronicle* supported the Republican Party as well. The *Patriot* was an on-again, off-again Democratic Party–leaning newspaper. Until the Civil War, two-party government prevailed. But the Republican Party dominated after the war. Democrats were blamed for the rebellion. The Republican Party was the party of Lincoln, abolition and victory. The local newspapers reflected all that; the most popular papers were Republican.

Population growth and residential and commercial construction matched the industrial expansion. The population had nearly doubled since 1870, and the city issued more than two hundred building permits in 1888.

CHURCH CONSTRUCTION

During the time of its greatest prosperity, Bridgeton invested heavily in church construction. By 1895, the town had twenty-four churches, fifteen of them built between 1860 and 1895. The decision to build a house of worship was usually a conservative one. First, a congregation was organized, and then it built a chapel. Then the church proper was built, often years later. Sometimes a church was built only after a congregation had developed in the form of a regularly attended prayer meeting.

Until the Victorian building boom, the number of churches was small. The earliest church was the Broad Street Presbyterian Church, followed by the Commerce Street Methodist Episcopal Church (First Methodist) in 1807 and the First Baptist Church, originally Pearl Street Baptist Church, in 1816. The First Presbyterian Church on North Laurel Street was built in 1836. Three years later, the Second Presbyterian Church was built by a group that thought the town could support another Presbyterian church. The Mount Zion African Methodist Episcopal Church built a chapel in 1855.

Then, in the 1860s, a group from the First Presbyterian Church, with a handful of supporters from the Second Presbyterian Church, determined to build a church on the west side of town. They began modestly, with the chapel of the West Presbyterian Church (now First Presbyterian Church) built in 1869. Construction continued, with some pauses, probably for fundraising, until 1878.

In 1866, Bridgeton Presbyterians built the Pearl Street Mission for the latchkey children of the time. The mission offered Bible study and Sunday school programs for such children. There were night school classes for working children.

Central Methodist Church looked much the same in 1916 as it does in 2012. *Courtesy of Claire Biggs.*

Congregations of Lutherans, Episcopalians and Roman Catholics built their first churches in Bridgeton during the Victorian decades. Before the various denominations could meet in their own buildings, they met in private homes or in public halls. More than one devotional group used Grosscup's Hall or Riley's Hall.

Churches built in Bridgeton during that period included:

St. Andrew's Episcopal Church: The first services were held in July 1864, although the building was not finished.

St. Mary's Roman Catholic Church: It was built in 1866 on North Pearl Street, on a rural site, surrounded by cornfields. Rural soon changed to urban as more homes were built in the neighborhood.

First Methodist Protestant Church: The North Laurel Street church was dedicated in 1860, and a parsonage was built in the late 1860s.

Central Methodist Episcopal Church: Members of the Commerce Street Methodist Church organized in 1864 and built a chapel in 1867, and the church was dedicated in 1894.

Second Methodist Protestant Church: It was built on South Avenue and dedicated in January 1889.

Fourth Methodist Episcopal Church: It began with a Sunday school building in 1888. The church was dedicated in 1889.

Wesley Memorial Methodist Episcopal Church, North Pearl Street, shown here in 1911. The church burned down in 1915 and was completely rebuilt in stone. *Courtesy of Claire Biggs.*

WESLEY MEMORIAL METHODIST EPISCOPAL CHURCH: This wooden church building was dedicated in 1892. It burned down in 1915 and was completely rebuilt with stone.

EAST BRIDGETON METHODIST EPISCOPAL CHAPEL: This building began existence in 1887 as a Presbyterian chapel used for prayer meetings in the neighborhood. In 1893, the Methodist churches of Bridgeton bought it for their use. It never developed into a full-time church.

ST. JOHN'S GERMAN LUTHERAN CHURCH: The congregation met in Grosscup's Hall and Sheppard's Hall beginning in 1858. The church was built in 1869. Services were conducted in German.

CHRIST'S ENGLISH LUTHERAN CHURCH: The church was built in 1893.

BEREAN BAPTIST CHURCH: This church began as a Sunday school chapel in 1872 for members of the First Baptist Church and was formally organized as a congregation in 1893.

SOUTH BAPTIST CHAPEL: This was another Sunday school for the congregation of First Baptist Church, established in 1870.

NORTH PEARL STREET BAPTIST CHAPEL: It began in 1886 as a Sunday school for Pearl Street Baptist Church.

THIRD BAPTIST CHURCH: Black members of the Pearl Street Baptist Church formed a separate congregation in 1886, but they had no building and used public halls and the Berean Baptist chapel for services.

Pearl Street Mission and Fourth Presbyterian Church: The mission house was built in 1866 and developed into a separate congregation.

Irving Avenue Presbyterian Church: Members of Second Presbyterian Church and residents of the Irving Avenue neighborhood built this church in 1893.

CHURCH ARCHITECTURE

When Bridgeton congregations made the decision to build churches, they employed prominent architects. Samuel Sloan and Frank Watson, Philadelphia architects, both contributed to the design of Berean Baptist Church. Sloan and James Sims, another Philadelphia firm, was responsible for West Presbyterian Church. The trend for architectural quality probably began with the construction of the William G. Nixon house on Commerce Street in 1851. Thomas U. Walter, known for his work on the Capitol Rotunda in Washington, D.C., and the Delaware River mansion Andalusia, designed that house. Smith and Conover, leading Bridgeton contractors, did much of the construction work during the boom years.

WEST JERSEY ACADEMY

For about sixty years, beginning in 1850, Bridgeton was known for its excellent private secondary schools. At the time, public schooling was not compulsory, and the majority of pupils in public schools attended only half the sessions. Most stayed just long enough to learn to read, write and do simple arithmetic. Public schools did not prepare students for college. Private schools provided education for the college-bound children of wealth and privilege.

In 1852, at the urging of Dr. Samuel Beach Jones, pastor of the First Presbyterian Church, Presbyterians of West Jersey began the West Jersey Academy for boys. The school occupied the block bounded by Broad and Lawrence Streets, West Commerce Street and West Avenue. West Jersey Academy was not a military school, but the curriculum included military drill. The school's only income came from tuition fees and gifts. It experienced constant financial difficulty. West Jersey Academy closed in 1910. In 1912, the Bridgeton Board of Education bought the building and grounds.

West Jersey Academy, a private school for boys, closed in 1910. The Broad Street School now occupies the same property. *Courtesy of Jim Fogle.*

Ivy Hall began as a private home and was renovated to become a school for girls and then a hospital and convalescent center. *Courtesy of Claire Biggs.*

IVY HALL

In 1861, Margaretta Little Sheppard converted her husband's large West Commerce Street home into Ivy Hall, a finishing school for girls. Before her marriage, she had been a teacher at the public school on Bank Street. Mrs. Sheppard and her husband, Isaac, added classrooms and dormitories to the house. Three of Mr. Sheppard's daughters from previous marriages became teachers at the school.

Ivy Hall Seminary attracted the daughters of well-to-do New Jersey families. At one time, Ivy Hall had thirty boarding students, in addition to many Bridgeton day students. The girls studied academic subjects, art, music, French and, most important of all, the social graces cherished by Victorian society.

In 1872, Mrs. Sheppard took a group of young people to Europe as an extension of the Ivy Hall education. One of her successors as principal was Miss Ada L. Howard, who later became the first president of Wellesley College.

After Ivy Hall Seminary closed, Dr. Reba Lloyd bought the building. She added bathrooms and modern heating and converted the building into a sanitarium, with room for twenty-five patients. Ivy Hall opened as a hospital in 1918.

THE SOUTH JERSEY INSTITUTE

The South Jersey Institute was the largest and best-known Bridgeton boarding school. The West Jersey Baptist Association established the coeducational school in 1865, unusual for its time. The institute opened in 1870 on a ten-acre plot on the southeast corner of Atlantic and Lincoln Streets, with grounds overlooking the river. Horatio J. Mulford and several members of his family donated the property and $10,000 toward the cost of the building. It was a large structure, five stories high and 157 feet across the front. It had accommodations for 125 students, as well as the necessary offices and reception rooms. The school was lighted by gas and equipped with the luxuries of bathrooms and steam heat.

The institute offered courses for college-bound students and aspiring teachers and businessmen. It prepared young women for public school teaching. During its first twenty-five years, one hundred male graduates entered the ministry, and many others went on to colleges such as Brown, Bucknell, Colby, Lafayette and Cornell. Over five hundred institute graduates became public school teachers. Students came to the institute from all parts of the United States and South America.

Male students were required to participate in military drills and wear uniforms, though the school was not a military academy. Drills were considered an excellent form of exercise and the discipline a valuable aid in the formation of a manly character. Enrollment at the institute declined when public high schools began to offer college preparatory courses. The school closed in 1907, and the building was later demolished.

SEVEN GABLES SCHOOL

Seven Gables. Like Ivy Hall, this Victorian building began life as a home and was soon transformed into a school for girls. *Courtesy of Jim Bergmann.*

In 1886, Mrs. Sarah S. Westcott founded Seven Gables School for girls at her home on Lake Street. Seven Gables was built in a grove of tall oak trees, with wide lawns and grounds extending to Jeddy's Pond. The girls kept fit by walking along the banks of the raceway, rowing on its water or ice skating on Jeddy's Pond in the winter.

In 1919, Seven Gables became Lakeview Hospital, a private hospital. Later, the hospital shifted its emphasis to "nervous cases or persons suffering slightly from mental troubles."[51]

DAME SCHOOLS

Younger children attended small schools called "dame" schools. Bridgeton had several: Miss Minnie Red Ware's kindergarten and select school, located in the chapel of the First Presbyterian Church on the corner of Church Lane and North Pearl Street; the Ivy Hall kindergarten taught by Miss Julia Peck; Miss Carrie M. Iredell's school on Lake Street; Miss M.C. Applegit's (or Applegate) East Lake School on Elmer Street; and the kindergarten of Mrs. E.C. Sunfield. Miss Iredell's roomy school building still stands behind her former home.

In the Victorian framework, these women were occupied at one of the few jobs considered proper for women. They were permitted to earn money at a limited number of activities like dressmaking, teaching music or conducting a private school. Such employment was permissible if it could be confined to the home, with the money involved appearing to be a minor concern. The dame schools tended to be very tiny and could accommodate very few pupils. They were probably the Victorian version of kindergarten.

This building, known as Dame Howell's School, was relocated to the city park. It was a schoolhouse for very young children, an early kindergarten. *Photo by Sam Feinstein.*

HEALTH AND CULTURE

Health and cultural facilities were not so widely known but were just as important to local residents. Bridgeton women led the drive for a municipal hospital, which opened on Irving Avenue in 1899.

Moore's Opera House on South Laurel Street became the center of Bridgeton culture in the 1880s. The opera house could seat one thousand patrons. Professional entertainers and the Bridgeton Musical Union, a ninety-member community chorus, appeared at the Opera House. The Union performed Handel's "Messiah" and other concert programs. A Philadelphia acting troupe gave the first professional performance there in 1880. YMCA lectures, political meetings and commencement exercises were held there.

Fraternal organizations like the Masons, Odd Fellows, Knights of Pythias and Red Men dominated social life of the time. They combined entertainment and benevolent functions. Many of the secret societies served as private insurance companies, too.

City government began to offer up-to-date services, with prodding from voters. The Bridgeton Water Works began operation in December 1877. After a fire the previous winter, citizens voted overwhelmingly to approve a municipal water system. They also demanded and received a town fire engine. The public water was "the purest spring water quality" and obtained from wells and basins.[52] The pumping station and reservoirs were built in the vicinity of East Lake at a cost of $70,000. Bridgetonians celebrated the municipal pump priming with a parade on December 24.

Streetlights arrived in 1857 with the establishment of the Bridgeton Gas-Light Company on Water Street. Electricity, for evening hours only, was available for the first time in 1886. In 1898, the Bridgeton Electric Company built a new generating plant on Cohansey Street that provided service twenty-four hours a day. The company owned all electric lamps and renewed them when they burned out. Customers were required to apply for service in person.[53]

Given the municipal amenities and obvious prosperity, the Board of Trade sought to promote Bridgeton's advantages:

> *Extensive manufacturing interests, an excellent shipping point, both by rail and water. Low freight and express charges. Fine passenger service. A most desirable residence city. Mild climate and high degree of healthfulness. Excellent system of waterworks. Schools unexcelled anywhere. Many and well-attended churches. Large and busy stores. An intelligent, prosperous*

Volunteer firefighters at the original Washington Street firehouse, located near the Cumberland Nail and Iron Works, shown in the 1890s. *Courtesy of Jim Bergmann.*

class of citizens. Beautiful and fertile surrounding country. Two staunch, well-managed banks. Building associations of highest standard. Electric railways and electric lights. Many villages immediately surrounding. Good government and orderly character.[54]

CHAPTER 6

CHANGING TIMES

At the beginning of the twentieth century, Bridgeton was a bustling industrial and mercantile center. Bridgetonians worked hard, but they played hard too. Nobody could complain, "There's nothing to do here." There was plenty to do, and it all started with the park.

The Bridgeton City Park developed from the generosity of the Cumberland Nail and Iron Works, the town's first dominant industry. The plant closed in 1899, a victim of industrial progress. During the years of its success, the company provided more than financial stability. It gave Bridgetonians an unofficial public park.

Bridgeton City Park, Lovers' Walk, 1908. This path is a favorite of Bridgetonians a century after this picture was made. *Courtesy of Claire Biggs.*

In the early 1800s, Ebenezer Seeley, James Lee and Smith Bowen had built Tumbling Dam on the Cohansey River for their mill north of town, and in the process, they formed Sunset Lake. The Reeves brothers, owners of the Nail Works, purchased the water power of that dam and built their own dam and raceway, thus creating Crystal Lake (Jeddy's Pond or Muddy Run).

BRIDGETON'S CROWN JEWEL

Residents used the Nail Works property for leisurely pursuits like picnics, fishing and pleasant strolls. In 1903, the city bought the land for $40,000. Most residents supported this acquisition, and Oberlin Smith was among them. The editor of the *Bridgeton Pioneer*, George McCowan, and Judge William A. Logue and Frank M. Riley led the support for purchase of the parkland. But opponents thought the price was too high. The critics were overruled, and the property east of West Avenue became public land. When the $40,000 bond issue was paid off in 1927, the property's value was estimated at $500,000.[55] In 1914, resident Mary Elmer had bequeathed a plot of family property to the city with the proviso that it be called Elmer Park. This land, west of West Avenue, included Mary Elmer Lake. Ananias Irelan formed the lake when he built a dam across Northwest Branch, a stream that emptied into the Cohansey and furnished power for his mill in the eighteenth century.

These two parcels were combined to form the main part of Bridgeton's prized park. The city also maintained Park Farm in the area of the current high school playing fields. Income from the farm helped to pay for upkeep and improvement of the grounds. After the waterworks was moved from East Lake to the west side of the river around 1910, that area was absorbed into the park system as Water Works Park.

With admirable foresight, officials consulted a New York landscape engineer for advice on proper development of the Nail Works parcel. The expert concluded that the area should be left in its natural state, with its abundance of oak, holly and laurel.[56] Regional author George Agnew Chamberlain described the park's charms in his 1924 novel, *The Lantern on the Plow*: "Lily pads—a closed lily bud, thrusting up its pointed nose. The climbing iridescent bubbles from some tadpole turning over in his bed of mud. A floating twig, with a leaf set for a sail, bound on some Lilliputian voyage at the mercy of minute unfelt drafts of air. Her eyes left all else to follow its fortunes."[57]

Water Works Building and the bridge connecting it to the city park, about 1910. *Courtesy of Claire Biggs.*

The park, with its one thousand acres of woodland, lakes and zoo, continues to delight residents and nonresidents alike. In 2012, this Bridgeton asset is the largest municipal park in South Jersey, and its value to the community cannot be measured.

In addition to the main park site, the city owned some smaller land parcels earmarked for public recreation. Clement W. Shoemaker donated land on North Laurel Street, known as Cumberland Park, for the use of employees of the Cumberland Glass Manufacturing Company. In later years, Owens-Illinois Glass Co. used it as a parking lot. Memorial Field, now the site of city hall, was a gift from a citizens' group that wanted to establish a memorial to Bridgeton's soldiers. The property was a popular baseball field during the sports heyday.

TUMBLING DAM PARK

Tumbling Dam Park was just across the city line in Deerfield Township (now Upper Deerfield Township) and was easily accessible by a local trolley line. It began as a private venture in 1893 and remained in private hands as it developed into a recreation center next to the city park. It featured an amusement park with rides, a bowling alley and a partially covered open-air

Tumbling Dam Park at the southeast corner of East Lake opened in 1894. Swimming was just one of the summertime activities at the park. It was a recreation center with an amusement park and rides, bowling alley, open-air theater and facilities for meetings and dinners. *Courtesy of Jim Bergmann.*

theater first called the Amusement Palace and then the Casino. A restaurant and canoe rental service were added enticements.

Regular trolleys took passengers to Tumbling Dam Park until 1922. During the 1920s, the park was a favored meeting place for the local Ku Klux Klan (aka the Kumberland Kounty Klan). In 1934, Marvin Rempfer bought Tumbling Dam Park. The public zoo was established that year, too.

That August, the worst flood in the city's history spilled through the area. Sheets of rain fell on the city during the night of August 2, 1934, and into the next day. The dam broke at Mary Elmer Lake, beginning a chain reaction that sent water into and over Sunset Lake and beyond. The *Dollar Weekly News* described the devastation: "[The] entire watershed of the western Cumberland County area gave way to a torrential rush, wiping out three bridges, destroying city water works properties, and inundating the business section of Bridgeton."[58] The surge pulled the oyster schooner *C.J. Peterson* from its moorings, and it smashed into the Commerce Street Bridge. Small buildings on the river collapsed, and residents of the downtown area were evacuated from their homes and businesses. This storm occurred during low tide and at a time when much of the country was suffering from a drought. The flood damaged Tumbling Dam Park, but it was rebuilt, along with the dams and bridges.

In the late 1920s, Rempfer and Leon Cassidy created a popular and long-lasting amusement park ride called the Pretzel. The ride was featured at Tumbling Dam Park and hundreds of other amusement parks throughout the United States. Production of the Pretzel continued until 1980, with a brief hiatus during World War II, when materials were scarce.

In 1941, Rempfer converted the open-air theater into a roller-skating rink, and five years later, a fire destroyed it.[59] A hurricane smashed the floating band shell he built in 1944. Flood, fire and storm convinced Rempfer to quit the park business, so he sold his property off for building lots in the 1950s. The resulting streets were named for members of his family.

SPORTS AND COMPETITION

Sporting events were popular activities in the city park as well. Canoe races and parades, swimming races, diving competitions and a marathon were all held there.

Team sports enjoyed tremendous popularity throughout the Bridgeton of the early twentieth century. Both South Jersey Institute and West Jersey Academy stressed athletics. A fierce rivalry developed between them. In 1906, South Jersey Institute played and defeated basketball teams from Brown Preparatory School, the University of Pennsylvania Dental School, Temple College and West Jersey Academy.

Local interest in athletics fostered the growth of semi-professional teams. In 1896, a group of young men organized the Bridgeton Athletic Association (BAA), the first athletic association in New Jersey. The BAA built its own gymnasium on the riverbank at the corner of Broad and Laurel Streets with facilities for baseball, basketball and bowling. Bridgeton High School teams played their basketball games there. The BAA continued a strong program through the 1920s and '30s.

Another athletic club, the Woodside Athletic Association, started in 1907 and continued until 1920, although its membership was drastically reduced after World War I. Woodside was known for its semi-professional basketball teams and won many local and state championships. At the height of its popularity, Woodside had three hundred members who played basketball, bowling and billiards in the Johnson Building on North Laurel Street. At various times they also used the Armory or the Hippodrome, which was a stadium and hall at Memorial Field.

Woodside and BAA competed in a Thanksgiving marathon every year. Woodside had baseball and track teams and a football team that played one game a year against BAA. The BAA sponsored a dinner each New Year's Day for hundreds of needy children. Woodside entertained the community with an annual minstrel show.

Another community gymnasium was part of the Moose Building on South Laurel Street.

Canoe parades and races were popular events at Bridgeton City Park in the first decades of the twentieth century. *Courtesy of Claire Biggs.*

The Crescent Canoe Club, circa 1916, one of many canoe clubs that used the Bridgeton park waters for their sport. *Courtesy of Jean Stelmach.*

Organized recreation for children lagged behind the adult activities. In 1912, the children of the city had one playground on East Avenue. In the 1930s, playgrounds were built on Monroe Street, South Avenue and Vine Street.

ENTERTAINMENT FOR ALL

Movie theaters appeared early in the twentieth century. A few years after renovations in 1901, Moore's Opera House became a movie theater called the Criterion. It could seat over 1,100 people and offered silent movies and musical and theatrical productions. The Woodside shows and concerts and plays by other amateur groups were held there too.

Well-known personalities appeared at the Criterion. John Philip Sousa and his band played there, Booker T. Washington lectured there and Woodrow Wilson stopped there during his campaign for governor.

The Majestic, at the corner of North Laurel Street and Church Lane, opened in 1911. The Stanley Theater showed the first talking motion pictures in Bridgeton in 1928. The Stanley was on the corner of Commerce and Pearl Streets, the present location of the local newspaper the *News of Cumberland County.*

Theaters entertained their patrons thoroughly. An evening's bill featured a movie, newsreel, travelogue and cartoon. Vaudeville singers, dancers, comedians, jugglers or acrobats performed on special Friday or Saturday nights.

The Stanley closed in 1951, and the Majestic showed its last film in 1958. The Criterion building was destroyed by fire in 1949. The theater reopened as the Laurel Theater in the mid-1950s. It closed, reopened and closed again.[60] Bridgeton no longer has a movie theater, and residents must drive more than ten miles to the nearest multiplex in Vineland.

A WAVE OF CHANGE

Bridgeton continued to ride the wave of Victorian prosperity, but its golden age ended in the 1920s. From its earliest days, the city had benefited from its position on the banks of the Cohansey River, its mild climate and willing workforce. Later, its location on the routes of two railroad lines reinforced the natural advantages. Those advantages diminished with the development of highways and the growth of trucking, factors in a twentieth-century urban

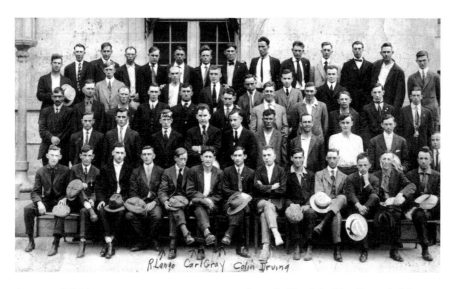

A group of Bridgeton-area young men prepare to leave for Fort Dix, New Jersey, in May 1918 to join the United States Army during World War I. *Courtesy of Jean Stelmach.*

economy. Even if the town had tried to isolate itself from the wider world—and it did not—it would have been unable to preserve its golden age and defend itself from change. It depended on the outside world for its prosperity.

The influenza epidemic of 1918 was a symbol of external forces at work in the early 1900s. Influenza killed at least 20 million persons worldwide, 675,000 in the United States. In October 1918, more than 4,300 Bridgetonians—out of a population of 14,209—had contracted influenza. Of these, 104 died from influenza and its accompanying pneumonia. The disease continued to spread for a few more months. But no period matched the virulence of that unhappy month when everybody was waiting for World War I to end.

Bridgeton's schools and churches were closed, and all public gatherings were outlawed until the worst of the epidemic had passed in early November. The disease claimed more victims than the war. Thirty-five local men died as a result of combat. But they knew they were risking their lives. Those who stayed home were unprepared for the insidious battle they faced.

Economic and social change hit Bridgeton with force equal to that of the epidemic, but the effects came gradually. When one community asset dwindled, another replaced it for a time.

Bridgeton's private schools did not survive long into the new century. By 1910, all had closed because public schools had begun to offer college

South Jersey Institute, Bridgeton's largest and only coeducational private school (1865–1907), on Atlantic Street, had lawns and playing fields that extended to the Cohansey River. *Courtesy of Jim Fogle.*

preparatory courses, which had been the purview of private schools. After 1907, the South Jersey Institute shut down permanently. The West Jersey Academy was sold to the public school system and became the site of Bridgeton High School, which became Bridgeton Junior High, then Bridgeton Middle School and now Broad Street School. Ivy Hall and Seven Gables became private sanitariums and maternity hospitals.

Bridgeton manufacturing profited from World War I. American industry needed Ferracute presses to make bullets and other armaments. Soldiers needed canned goods, uniforms and other products of Bridgeton's many factories.

After the war, Bridgeton supplied a civilian population with a vast array of products, from presses to bricks, buttons, tin cans, cigars, brass fixtures, garments of all kinds, candy, glass bottles, textiles and even ice. Local produce was processed in Bridgeton and featured peaches, apples, tomatoes, potatoes, spinach, cabbage and berries.

The social and cultural life was equally rich and full of choice. Twenty-six churches served the population. A seemingly limitless number of fraternal organizations, including two Masonic Lodges, welcomed male residents. The Odd Fellows, Knights of Pythias, Elks, Moose, Eagles, American Legion, Red Men and others were active. Four hundred women were members of the Civic Club. Music, study and cultural clubs were organized by and for women.

The Cumberland Hotel was built in 1923 to replace the old Cumberland Hotel on Laurel Street. The new one, on the corner of Pearl and Commerce Streets, was the finest in the county. It became a community center because of its ballroom, dining room and good food. The senior citizen high-rise building now occupies the site of the hotel.

Visitors and residents supported four hotels, two movie theaters, two daily newspapers and one public library. One eighty-five-bed hospital and three private hospitals tended the sick of the community. Two railroads, the New Jersey Central and the Pennsylvania Railroad, crossed the town. A trolley line connected Bridgeton and Millville, and two bus lines took passengers to Philadelphia and other points.

Four banks and six building and loan associations established a sturdy financial base, and 150 wholesale and retail stores offered their goods to the public. Eighty manufacturing plants, including seven canneries, three candy factories and one of the largest glass bottle plants in the country, operated in Bridgeton.

By the end of 1926, officials predicted, Bridgeton would have twenty miles of paved road within its borders.[61]

THE PROHIBITION ERA

From 1920 to 1933, the Eighteenth Amendment to the Constitution was in effect. Prohibition was the law of the land. Bridgeton had been "dry" before. The Ivy Hall catalogue of 1886 proclaimed, "The City of Bridgeton is noted for its morality and social refinement. No licenses are granted and there are no saloons. The quiet of the streets is often remarked upon."[62] In 1888, the whole county went dry and forbade the sale of intoxicating liquors. In 1911, Bridgetonians voted—556 to 158—to outlaw licensed bars. Members of the Woman's Christian Temperance Union (WCTU) and the Anti-Saloon League and other groups were overjoyed.

Support for national prohibition a decade later was muted. While Prohibition had its adherents, moonshine and less potent forms of illegal alcohol were available in Bridgeton, as elsewhere. Rumrunning was an acknowledged activity along the Delaware Bay–Cohansey River area. Sometimes the rum smugglers were forced to throw their cargo into the bay, and years later, boaters and fishermen found boxes of the stuff mired in the low-lying marshes.

Local readers were obviously intrigued by the illicit alcohol trade. The stock market crash of October 1929 was the most important national news. But the *Dollar Weekly News* ignored the event and featured a story on the breakup of an alcohol smuggling operation outside Atlantic City.

The town could not ignore the stock market crash or the Depression that followed. The Depression touched everybody, of course. Bridgeton's economic stability, conservatism and caution immunized residents, including local investors, against the most severe effects. Not one Bridgeton bank failed during the Depression. The only bank holidays observed in Bridgeton were those proclaimed by President Franklin Delano Roosevelt. The Cumberland Trust Company and the Cumberland National Bank merged during that time, but it was not considered a panic merger.

Some cities were forced to pay their teachers and civic employees with scrip, a form of voucher, instead of cash. Bridgeton continued to pay its teachers in cash throughout the Depression. Residents lived with hardship during those years. Some workers took pay cuts, and others suffered layoffs or loss of jobs, but life's necessities were available, provided by a rural economy.

THE KU KLUX KLAN

Bigotry and narrow-mindedness grew like weeds after World War I, leading up to and during the Depression. Perhaps hardship bred intolerance; perhaps intolerance was simply a reaction to change. Whatever the reason, the Ku Klux Klan was in full flower. The Klan pollinated hate and resentment toward Jews, blacks and Catholics. Klan members felt obliged to hide under their hooded sheets when they appeared in public places. But they still held meetings in well-known, well-attended spots. Bridgeton's reception of the Klan reveals the odd respectability attached to the group. However, in June 1924, when a crowd of about two hundred Klansmen tried to menace a black man in his cell at the Bridgeton jail, police sent them away without incident.

On July 26, 1924, hundreds of people attended a "Knighthawks Jubilee," a Klan gathering at Tumbling Dam Park. The all-day program featured a dinner at 2:00 p.m. and a baseball game between the American Legion and Port Norris teams. Bridgeton mayor Samuel C. Johnson led the group in a prayer, and a local minister gave a speech on "Americanism." During the festivities, three hundred men and two hundred women were inducted into Klan organizations.

It was the parade, however, that has remained in the community memory. That evening, led by a white-robed figure on horseback, adult men and women

Members of the Ku Klux Klan march openly in a public parade during the 1920s. *Courtesy of Jim Bergmann.*

and junior members of the Klan from Gloucester, Salem and Cumberland Counties marched or motored silently through the center of town and back to the park. The "Jubilee" ended in a display of fireworks at Tumbling Dam Park.

Ralph A. Brandt, longtime editor of the *Bridgeton Evening News*, claimed he could identify Klan members by their shoes because the robes did not hide footwear.

That April, the county Klan held a meeting outside Millville on the Cedarville Road. The crowd was estimated at six to ten thousand. There is no way to know how many were actually Klan members. The Klan was a secret society and controlled its own statistics. The group reported that several hundred new members were initiated that day. Fireworks ended that celebration too.[63]

Klan members, in full regalia, routinely marched in Bridgeton Decoration Day and Labor Day parades. If the KKK meant to scare and impress people with its parades and mass meetings, it succeeded. If the purpose was elimination of the groups opposed by the Klan, the histrionics were wasted.

GROWTH OF MINORITIES

Jewish, black and Catholic minorities were established parts of the community and were still growing. By 1929, blacks composed 12 percent of Bridgeton's population, according to Polk's 1928–29 Directory. Another 8 percent of Bridgeton residents were foreign-born, and the remainder were "native white."

Many of Bridgeton's black residents were descendants of Gouldtown's original families. They could trace their roots to colonial times and the Fenwick family. Blacks lived in neighborhoods around Vine Street and the small streets off East Avenue. They often worked as servants for white households.[64]

Jews first came to Cumberland County in the 1880s to escape religious persecution in Russia and Germany. They settled in rural areas and later moved to Bridgeton. In the early 1900s, the town had thirty Jewish families. They had no synagogue and, like their Christian counterparts, held religious services in public buildings. At first, the Horner Building (later known as the Steinbrook Building) offered temporary space. Then in 1915, temporary quarters on North Laurel Street became permanent. The cornerstone was laid that year, and in 1916, the synagogue was dedicated. In 1920, a Young Men's Hebrew Association (YMHA) was organized with headquarters on South Laurel Street. A short time later, the YMHA and the congregation merged. The growing membership needed more space for a religious school. In 1948, Mr. and Mrs. Max Feinstein donated the Pritchard Canning Company office building at Irving Avenue and North Pearl Street for that purpose.

Meanwhile, members began to plan the proposed Congregation Beth Abraham complex, which would include a school, auditorium and sanctuary. The first building, the Max Feinstein Memorial School of Congregation Beth Abraham, was dedicated in 1953. Three years later, the Max C. Schrank Auditorium was added, and ground for the new synagogue was broken on Purim 1970. Ionic Lodge No. 97 bought the original synagogue in 1962. The congregation used the Schrank auditorium for worship until the new building was ready.[65]

Bridgeton Roman Catholics waited for over a century before they had their own church. Catholics had resided in the town since it was Cohansey Bridge, years before the Revolution. Their original number is unknown, but it was probably very small. In those days, a traveling Jesuit came to town once or twice a year to celebrate Mass and perform baptisms and marriages. When St. Mary's was built in 1864, no more than thirty families made up the parish. St. Mary's parish changed its name to the Church of the Immaculate Conception in 1915. The parochial school was built in 1925, during the time of intense KKK activity. A second Roman Catholic church, St. Teresa of Avila, was founded in 1961.

AN INDUSTRIAL GIANT

In 1920, the Illinois Glass Company bought the Cumberland Glass Manufacturing Company. The Illinois Company installed automatic

The Owens-Illinois plant dominated the landscape in north Bridgeton in the 1950s, as it dominated the economy then. *Courtesy of Jim Bergmann.*

glassmaking equipment and thus began the gradual transition to modern glassmaking. At one time, the Bridgeton plant employed hundreds of highly skilled glassblowers. Their services were no longer needed when the process was fully automated.

In 1923, one factory was destroyed by fire. The company replaced it with a completely modern machine factory, which was the foundation of the physical plant of the future Owens-Illinois Co.

In 1929, the Owens Bottle Company merged with the Illinois company to form the Owens-Illinois Glass Company, the only glassworks in town. At its peak, from 1955 to 1976, Owens-Illinois employed as many as 2,500 workers to operate eight furnaces. At the time, the Bridgeton factory made four million bottles a day, more than any other glass factory.[66] By the time the plant closed in 1984, the workforce was down to 637 employees. Just two furnaces and five bottle-forming machines remained.

In the interim, Owens-Illinois became the single largest employer in Bridgeton's history. It influenced the city's recreational and charitable spheres as well. The company provided gifts that the whole community used and enjoyed, notably a ball field and bandstand. The company sponsored scout troops and sports activities and provided summer jobs for high school and college students. Needy employees benefited from a company welfare fund. The plant clubhouse had four bowling alleys and facilities for shuffleboard, basketball, ping-pong and bocce leagues. Owens-Illinois athletes played on softball teams and attended company sports banquets. The firm initiated some of these activities during the Depression but continued them long afterward.

P.J. RITTER COMPANY

The P.J. Ritter Company was the most important canning factory in Bridgeton throughout the twentieth century. The firm, known for processing fruits and vegetables, began in Bridgeton in 1915. For a while, Ritter's was Bridgeton's second-largest employer, with 1,000 to 1,200 workers. The company specialized in tomato products, especially juice and catsup. Its most notable product was the catsup, made from tons of the legendary Jersey tomatoes. During the summer, open trucks laden with the prized crop lined up all the way to Broad Street Cemetery and waited to enter the Ritter plant. The whole town was scented with the sweet-pungent smell of catsup.

TEXTILE MANUFACTURING

A succession of textile firms has occupied the site of the first local textile company, the East Lake Woolen Mill. Martin Dyeing and Finishing was there until 1948, when it went out of business. The Aberfoyle Textile Plant quickly replaced it. The Martin firm resumed its business, moved to Irving Avenue in 1948 and remains at the same location. Bridgeton Dyeing and Finishing replaced Aberfoyle in the 1950s and sold the building in 1985 to Inscon/Petro Cable. In the 1930s, Seibel and Stern employed 125 people to make children's clothing in a plant on Orchard Street.

AN AGRICULTURAL GIANT

Seabrook Farms was one of the leading food producers in the country during the twentieth century. The Seabrook plant was located just a few miles north of Bridgeton, and many Bridgetonians worked there. For most of its existence (1893–1959), Seabrook Farms was identified with C.F.

Seabrook Farms, shown in an aerial photograph in 1950. The tower in the center was the symbol of Seabrook. Employee housing is visible behind the tower. *Courtesy of Seabrook Educational and Cultural Center.*

(Charles Franklin) Seabrook, the "Henry Ford of Agriculture."[67] Though C.F. was a farmer from boyhood, he hated farming and dirt. Construction engineering was his consuming interest, so he applied engineering principles to his farming. He created an agribusiness.

Seabrook was an early user of overhead irrigation of crops. Since he did not depend on Mother Nature to water his plants, he was able to predict harvest time with some accuracy. Belford Seabrook, C.F.'s oldest son, improved on a method of quick-freezing vegetables invented by Clarence Birdseye. The company also developed its own seed varieties, which would yield the tastiest produce for freezing. Seabrook Farms began to process frozen vegetables in the late 1930s,[68] eventually turning out ninety million pounds a year.

Seabrook crops covered fifty thousand acres. The company owned about half the land; other farmers owned the rest.[69] At its busiest, from late March to late October, the company employed as many as 3,500 workers to grow, harvest and freeze spinach, peas, green beans, lima beans, corn, asparagus and strawberries, all at peak freshness.[70] Seabrook food fed the world and the troops during the two world wars.

C.F. built roads, houses, greenhouses and factory buildings at every opportunity. He built his own village for employees recruited from the West Indies, West Virginia, post–World War II refugee camps in Europe and Japanese American internment camps in the United States.

Workers at Seabrook Farms line up to receive their pay in silver dollars as the director of the mint, Nellie Taylor Ross, looks on, June 1950. *Courtesy of Seabrook Educational and Cultural Center.*

In June 1950, to demonstrate the impact of Seabrook Farms on the local economy, C.F. paid his 3,200 employees in silver dollars. The coins turned up all around the county; C.F. had proved his point.

The dark side of this marvel was its dependence on cheap labor. In April 1934, Jerry Brown, a black farmworker who was president of the aspiring Agricultural and Cannery Workers Industrial Union at Seabrook, led fellow workers, black and white, as they went on strike to protest low pay. They sought to double the hourly wage paid to women to twenty-five cents and the amount paid to men to thirty cents. The peaceful work stoppage ended when C.F. agreed to the raises. But in June, pleading his own lack of funds, he announced that the rates would be cut to twenty cents for men, eighteen cents for women and fifteen cents for children. In addition, he disregarded formerly agreed-upon seniority and laid off 125 workers, most of whom were black, Jerry Brown included.

Thus the second strike of 1934 followed quickly and was not peaceful. C.F. hired strikebreakers and used tear gas, nausea gas, clubs and fire hoses to subdue the strikers, who resorted to throwing rocks. Avowed Communist labor organizers had joined the fray on behalf of the workers, and C.F.

responded with charges of Communist influence and outside agitators, which was partially true by then. None of this could explain away the workers' poverty or the justice of their demands, however.

A delegation of strikers visited Secretary of Labor Frances Perkins in Washington, D.C., and asked for her help. She agreed to send a mediator. In a matter of days, U.S. Commissioner of Conciliation John A. Moffitt had arrived to settle the strike. Workers quickly accepted the terms, which required the rehiring of as many strikers as needed to fill jobs and the establishment of a board of adjustment to set wages and working conditions. The Communist organizers did not want to settle and left the area.[71] The union dissolved after that, but in 1941, Union Local 56, Meat and Cannery Workers, AFL, was established at Seabrook Farms. It was the first closed-shop contract for a farm in the United States.

Jack Seabrook, C.F.'s youngest son, said, "Once freezing commenced, Seabrook was the brightest spot in the economy of southern New Jersey."[72] That innovation of flash-freezing produce was introduced in the 1930s, after the strike. Seabrook wages and working conditions improved after that as well.

WORLD WAR II

World War II kept Bridgeton factories busy and the town's workers in demand. The DuPont Company of Delaware competed with Ferracute for skilled workers, many of whom were women.

The town mourned for the sixty-eight Bridgetonians who died for their country. Like the rest of the nation, the civilian population learned to make do with insubstantial rations of meat, butter, sugar, tires and gasoline. During the war, factories faced an acute labor shortage. Owens-Illinois recruited female workers from Pennsylvania and West Virginia. The community did not welcome the Owens-Illinois recruits or the Japanese Americans employed by Seabrook Farms. Descendants of both groups remain in the area and add their own spice to the Bridgeton population mix.

With a return to a postwar economy, Bridgeton's business climate changed for good. After the Civil War, prosperity spread like a contagion throughout the Northeast, and Bridgeton was not immune. One hundred years later, established industries forsook the region. Companies merged, consolidated or, worse, closed factories. They abandoned old plants and workers who had become too sophisticated in their demands for wages and benefits. Changing technology closed some of the factories too. Bridgeton's economic news reflected the fate of the Northeast. Between 1963 and 1983, Bridgeton lost four thousand jobs.

The Ferracute Machine Company closed in 1968, ending a chapter of benevolent management and inventive genius unmatched in the city's history. In the 1950s, Seabrook Farms employed 2,500 workers, many of them Bridgeton residents. In 1959, C.F. sold the company to Seeman Brothers. That firm lacked the foresight and drive of the Seabrook family, and Seabrook Farms stopped processing fresh vegetables in 1976. At that time, 500 workers were laid off, and 150 farmers had to sell their produce elsewhere. The P.J. Ritter Co. halted production in 1975 and sold the plant in 1976. The move cut 40 full-time workers and a large number of summer workers. Owens-Illinois cut its workforce by 700 in 1978, and by 1979, Owens-Illinois had just 1,000 employees, less than half its peak force. The company left Bridgeton in 1984.

In 1936, Price Brothers Lithograph Company opened in Bridgeton and employed two hundred skilled and semi-skilled workers in its best years. The company closed its doors in 1976. Two hundred people lost their jobs when Hunt Foods left in 1982. Stevcoknit closed the Murbeck plant and Bridgeton Dyeing and Finishing, which had employed two hundred people. The Stevcoknit plant at the corner of East Avenue and East Commerce Streets was sold in 1985.

Many Bridgetonians were convinced that they lived in a dying town. Racial disturbances in the high school in 1971 seemed to deliver the final blow. Some thought the dying began with "the troubles at the high school." A report on the disturbances concluded that racial tensions were a symptom, not a cause, of community malaise. Furthermore, bitter competition between the races for the few available jobs was a reflection of the town's economic reality. Employers constantly imported groups of poor, uneducated workers needed for the mostly unskilled and semi-skilled jobs.[73] Each new group replaced the last as the economic and social scapegoat.

Bridgeton, a once proud industrial city, clung to fading industries based on agricultural production. High unemployment sundered an already disjointed populace. The town's prospects looked grim.

CHAPTER 7

ENDURING INSTITUTIONS

Throughout decades of economic ebb and flow, Bridgeton Hospital and Bridgeton Free Public Library endured. Both were formed because of the dedication and persistence of small groups of determined citizens. In 1898, a group of concerned women began to work to establish a community hospital, the first hospital in the area.

WOMEN LEAD THE WAY

Elizabeth Hoffman Reeves (Mrs. Charles F.) initiated the effort with a speech before the Seven Oaks Club. Members of the Seven Oaks Club and the Katherine E. More Sick Fund Society soon set up a temporary Bridgeton Hospital Association. The women adopted the following resolution: "That no matter where or how the enterprise originated, it is the purpose of its founders to make it entirely cosmopolitan. The Hospital is to minister to the needs of all races, creeds, and conditions."[74]

They took their cause to Bridgeton's men of business and industry, many of whom were their husbands. The Seven Oaks Club is an active organization in 2012.

The association purchased the R.D. Cole property on Irving Avenue, made necessary repairs to the house and opened a ten-bed hospital in June 1899. The hospital had an operating room, two three-bed wards, one two-bed room and two private rooms. This was financed through a down payment of $250 and a $2,500 mortgage.

In 1900, the hospital established a training school for nurses, which continued for forty years.

Bridgeton Hospital as it appeared in 1910. The original building is at right, and the brick annex is at left. *Courtesy of Jim Bergmann.*

After a community-wide fund drive, hospital supporters raised $246,000 to build a new four-story, eighty-five-bed hospital, dedicated in 1926. Whenever funds were needed, the women worked to raise them. There is no doubt that without the women, and especially Elizabeth Reeves, there would be no hospital. But as the hospital became a reality, the women deferred to men. They had to wait for male approval to form an auxiliary group.

Through the years, the Women's Auxiliary raised funds for several additions to the hospital. In 1958, the Magnolia Avenue addition provided an additional sixty-five beds; operating, recovery and delivery rooms; and a pediatrics department. More quarters for patients were added in the 1960s, and the new radiology department was completed.

The six-story Winfield More Tower Wing added 140 more medical-surgical beds, an enlargement of the obstetrics department and a 10-bed intensive care unit in 1973. At that time, the pediatrics and surgery departments were also upgraded. The George J. Geisinger Surgical Center and a 29-bed mental health unit were added in the following decade. The Irving Avenue School was transformed into a renal dialysis unit in that period. Then, in the 1980s, the hospital needed more room. In 1985, the two-story East Wing added a medical-surgical section, conference rooms, a patients' lounge, a new main lobby and offices.

Bridgeton Hospital was the oldest hospital in the county and the most financially sound. With all the additions, it became the largest one in Cumberland and Salem Counties, with beds for 252 patients.

MEDICAL CARE CHANGES

In 1987, the Bridgeton and Millville Hospitals began to combine services and established Cooperative Health Care of Southern New Jersey (CHC). By doing so, they were able to "provide a broader range of patient services, cost savings, shared technology and management, and greater financial stability and flexibility in meeting the changing complexities of health care services."[75] They were responding to the transformation of medical care in the 1980s. Changes in medical practice, such as laparoscopic surgeries, reduced the time that patients spent in the hospital. Occupancy rates declined, and the need for hospital beds decreased.

Payment for healthcare was changing, too. Insurance companies, Medicare and Medicaid underpaid their hospital bills and pressured hospitals to shorten patient stays. In addition, HMOs and physician-run programs competed with hospitals for patients. Hospitals everywhere struggled to survive. In New Jersey, twenty-four hospitals closed between 1992 and 2008, and five filed for bankruptcy in 2007, including Kessler Memorial Hospital in Hammonton.

A REGIONAL MEDICAL CENTER

A group of officials from the Bridgeton and Millville Hospitals viewed consolidation of services as the way to maintain hospital care for Cumberland County residents. Public sentiment opposed the move because people did not want to lose their hometown hospitals. But hospital leaders saw the risk of inaction. They were as concerned about providing for the health of residents as Elizabeth Reeves and her colleagues had been ninety years earlier. Paul Cooper, president and chief executive officer of Bridgeton Hospital; Elizabeth "Betty" Miller, chair of Millville Hospital; and Thomas G. Roberts, chairman of the board of directors of Bridgeton Hospital, were instrumental in creating the merger.

The success of the Bridgeton-Millville effort paved the way. From 1993 to 2003, through mergers with Elmer Hospital and Newcomb Hospital of

Vineland and several name and structural changes, Cooperative Health Care of Southern New Jersey developed into the system known as South Jersey Healthcare. The goal of all the mergers was a new regional hospital, which would require approval from the State of New Jersey and the Federal Trade Commission. Approval was granted. The cities of Bridgeton and Millville created obstacles to the proposal when they filed separate suits against the plan. Both lawsuits failed.[76]

Regional cooperation finally prevailed, and the 325-bed Regional Medical Center was built in Vineland at Sherman Avenue and College Drive. It opened in August 2004, located close to the geographic center of the county and placed to serve residents of all the county's cities. Elmer Hospital serves its area of Salem County, as well as Cumberland County.

Bridgeton Hospital continues to provide medical care as part of the South Jersey Healthcare network under a new name, the Bridgeton Health Center. It provides a host of services, including emergency care; kidney dialysis; inpatient and outpatient behavioral (mental) healthcare for children, adolescents and adults; physical and occupational therapy; imaging and laboratory services; and a short-term hospice center whose purpose is to return patients to their nursing homes or their own homes. The volunteer office and a fitness center are also located in the building.

Many of the business functions of South Jersey Healthcare are in Bridgeton, including the finance department, computer system, medical records office, marketing and public relations, human resources and payroll. About 500 employees work at the Bridgeton facility full time or part time. South Jersey Healthcare employs 3,320 people throughout the whole system and 2,850 in the county. It is the county's largest employer.

DR. MARY BACON

When Dr. Mary Bacon opened an office in Bridgeton in 1918, the influenza epidemic was at its worst and some local doctors were gone, serving in World War I. Patients welcomed her care, but a few of the remaining doctors—all men of course—would not accept a female doctor under any circumstances. They excluded her from the Bridgeton Hospital staff for two decades, until 1939. During that period, her friends among the local doctors admitted patients to the hospital for her when it was necessary. Dr. Bacon did not let herself become bitter. It was not her first encounter with rejection, and the health of patients was her main concern.

Dr. Mary Bacon, shown upon her graduation from Woman's Medical College of Pennsylvania in 1916. *Courtesy of Mary Caruthers Cossaboon.*

She had expressed a desire to become a doctor when she was a teenager. Her grandmother opposed the plan because it was a scandalous choice for a young woman of the time. "I feel sorry for your father," she said. "You are the only child and look how you are turning out." The fact that Mary was the first girl born in the Bacon family in 257 years might have inspired her grandmother's opposition. But Mary's parents supported her, and she enrolled at Woman's Medical College of Pennsylvania and graduated in 1916. She served an internship at West Philadelphia Hospital for Women the following year.

Dr. Bacon made frequent house calls, often with her husband, J. Irving Caruthers, driving the car. He quit his job in a glass factory to run the household and act as her driver. She delivered generations of babies in Bridgeton and the surrounding townships and traveled as far as Mullica Hill to visit patients. She kept long office hours. Patients returned her affection. Everybody in town and out called her "Dr. Mary." She never lost her zest for the practice of medicine. In the November 1947 issue of *We Women* magazine, she wrote:

The practice of medicine is "A Way of Life," not (except coincidentally—certainly not primarily) a means of livelihood. It is an avocation at the same time that one practices it as a vocation. There is more tragedy, more human interest, more entertainment, more comedy in one day in the practice of medicine, than in a whole combined season of Broadway successes.

She became president of the hospital staff that had rejected her and president of the Cumberland County Medical Society. When Leonard Scott, MD, an African American doctor, arrived in Bridgeton, Dr. Mary welcomed and supported him. He, too, was shunned by medical colleagues and forced to wait about twenty years, until 1958, before he was accepted on staff at Bridgeton Hospital. Dr. Mary admitted patients to the hospital for him, as had been done for her years earlier.

In 1969, Dr. Mary was the first woman to receive the Doctor of the Year award from the Academy of Medicine of New Jersey. She received the Golden Merit Award from the Cumberland County Medical Society for her fifty years in medical practice. In 1967, the New Jersey Medical Women's Association honored as her as Woman Physician of the Year. She received the Sportsman Corner trophy in 1966 for her service to sports and recreation in the city of Bridgeton and the Huck Finn Award for outstanding service to youth. She was an avid football fan, and for years, she made sure a physician (often herself) was in attendance at Midget League football games. She also served on the New Jersey Medical Society's committee for maternal and infant welfare for thirty years.

She continued to practice obstetrics until she was seventy-five and maintained her general medical practice until her death of a heart attack at seventy-seven. Her husband died exactly one year later, in 1972. Their daughter, Mary Caruthers Cossaboon, is the sole surviving member of the immediate family.

BRIDGETON FREE PUBLIC LIBRARY

Bridgeton's library began much earlier than the hospital, in 1811. Men established the library, and Bridgeton women kept it going. The Bridgeton Library Company had thirty-seven stockholders, mainly business and professional men. President of the trustees was General Ebenezer Elmer. The company maintained the library in his medical office at the corner of Commerce and Orange Streets.

The company continued until 1854, when the trustees voted to donate the library to the West Jersey Academy. In 1859, a library was added to the new Bridgeton YMCA, and in 1886, Bridgeton women organized a ladies' auxiliary to direct the library. When the YMCA was dissolved in 1894, the women took complete charge of the community library. In 1901, they bought the 1816 Cumberland Bank building and founded the Bridgeton Library Association, which ran the subscription library for twenty years. The women sponsored concerts, socials and lectures to raise money to augment the modest subscription fees.

In 1921, the subscription library was discontinued and changed into a free public library, solely supported by donations and fundraising. But library trustees recognized the difficulty of trying to maintain the library without guaranteed income, so they went to city officials for help.[77] Support for the library was put before the voters, and in 1922, Bridgetonians overwhelmingly approved city financing for the library. When that was accomplished, state rules required the City of Bridgeton to provide operating funds for the library. That financial obligation continues even now.

In 1967, new construction expanded the size of the library. Offices, workrooms and the library's New Jersey collection were moved into the old building. That same year, a volunteer group called Friends of the Library was established. That group promoted community support for the library through special programs and raised money with a schedule of concerts and book sales until the late 1980s.

As industry left Bridgeton and city revenues fell, in the 1980s, mayors began to suggest closing the library as a way to cut costs. Meanwhile, residents relied even more on library services, especially computer use and Internet access. The library endured with reduced staff and hours. Then the recession of 2008 hurt an already struggling city and library. Library hours were reduced again, as were employee hours, and the payroll shrank. In 2012, the library staff is smaller than in the past, with just four full-time employees and several part-time employees.

In 2003, the Friends of the Bridgeton Library was reestablished. Concerned citizens founded Save the Library! in response to its possible closing in 2009. In partnership with the older group, Save the Library! initiated a campaign to raise funds to restore the historic building. The successful effort has financed replacement of the roof and other vital repairs toward eventual complete restoration of the structure. The Friends group has also continued its financial support for library programming and materials and recent purchase of youth computers. What the groups do in the future could depend on the needs of the library.

Since 1923, when the library became a municipal responsibility, Bridgeton mayors have appointed a library board of trustees, with the mayor and superintendent of schools serving as ex-officio members. Debbi Boykin-Greenberg is the current president of the trustees. Gail Robinson has been director of the library since 1993.

Throughout its years as a municipal service, the library has received the state-mandated appropriation from the city, with additional funds to meet its budget. In fiscal year 2011, the city eliminated all but the minimum appropriation, leaving the future of the library in doubt. The allotment is a fixed percentage of city revenue and is not based on library costs. It falls short of paying for all library expenses. The library board does have limited private funds, but they could be exhausted in a year or two, and the library's safety net would be gone. This financial struggle recalls the difficulty the library endured before it became a municipal responsibility ninety years ago. The future of the Cumberland County Library is in doubt, also, as the freeholders search for ways to pare costs for the county. Given town and county economic distress, the future of both libraries is uncertain.

Despite the uncertainty, the ever-helpful Bridgeton staff maintains library services. Books, magazines, DVDs and audiotapes are available to check out, but the choice is limited by decreased funds. Computers, fax and copy machines, digital resources, downloadable books and audiobooks are well used by the citizenry. Activities for children and teens include book discussions, crafts, a cooperative program between teens and younger children and a weekly teen program supported by Community Block Grant funds. Staff members also conduct the Children's Story Hour, a weekly library feature since 1928.

Patrons continue to attend monthly adult book discussions, teen meetings and anime movie nights and special programs and visit the Woodruff Museum in the lower level of the library. The museum features an extensive collection of Lenni-Lenape artifacts.

CHAPTER 8

CITY GOVERNMENT

Consolidation joined Bridgeton on the east side of the Cohansey River and Cohansey Township on the west side into the city of Bridgeton, incorporated in 1865. James Hood was elected as the first mayor. Councilmen representing the wards of the city took office at the same time. They were Charles S. Fithian, David P. Mulford, Robert C. Nichols, Thomas U. Harris, Samuel Applegate and Robert J. Fithian.

In 1875, the city charter was amended to the point that a new charter was actually devised. It gave the mayor and the common council the power to pass ordinances. Seth P. Husted was the first mayor under the 1875 "charter." The voters approved a formal charter in 1907. This charter gave city council the power to hire a commissioner of public works and buildings; a commissioner of streets, highways and parks; and a commissioner of public safety for one-year terms. Later, tenure for elected and appointed officials increased to three-year terms. George Hampton, a former mayor, served as the first mayor under this charter. Although it was an administrative innovation, this charter established a weak mayor-council system that proved to be inefficient.

In 1968, Bridgeton voters authorized a study of the charter and elected a commission to do the studying. The commission concluded that the weak mayor-council system was detrimental to day-to-day operation of the city and the needs of residents. The mayor was severely limited in authority, and council maintained loose ties to municipal offices. Nobody was in charge. Changes had to be made. A year later, voters approved a system known as Plan A under the Faulkner Act. Plan A sets up a strong mayor-council government and calls for a nonpartisan election every four years in May.

The nonpartisan nature of the election of mayor and council is theoretical. Since the inception of Plan A, the major parties have supported slates of candidates. Candidates do not use formal party designations but, rather, slogans chosen for their campaigns. Bertram R.B. Aitken, the first mayor elected under Plan A in 1970, was a Republican supported by the Republican Party.

SECRETARY OF AGRICULTURE DOUGLAS H. FISHER

In 2012, the most prominent state official from Bridgeton is Douglas H. Fisher, New Jersey secretary of agriculture. He was appointed by the New Jersey Board of Agriculture under Democratic governor Jon Corzine in 2009. Governor Chris Christie chose to keep him on in his Republican administration. Fisher began his career in public service on Bridgeton City Council in 1989. After that, he was elected to the Cumberland County Board of Freeholders for ten years, several years as freeholder director. From 2001 to 2009, he was assemblyman for the Third Legislative District, which covers Cumberland, Salem and Gloucester Counties. During his time in the Assembly, he was deputy majority whip and chair of the Agriculture and Natural Resources Committee.

He sponsored farmland, open space and preservation bills. His selection as New Jersey secretary of agriculture in 2009 was a natural one, given the rural district he represented in the Assembly and his work on behalf of New Jersey agriculture. He was named Outstanding Conservation Legislator in 2007 by the New Jersey Association of Conservation Districts and received a distinguished service award from the New Jersey Farm Bureau in 2005. As secretary of agriculture, he promotes expansion of the state's Jersey Fresh and Jersey Grown programs.

New Jersey Secretary of Agriculture Douglas H. Fisher. *Courtesy of New Jersey Department of Agriculture.*

ASSEMBLYWOMAN CELESTE M. RILEY

Celeste M. Riley of Bridgeton is the first woman to represent the Third Legislative District of New Jersey. She was appointed in 2009 to complete the unexpired term of Douglas H. Fisher when he resigned to become New Jersey secretary of agriculture. Assemblywoman Riley was reelected in 2011. She had been a member of Bridgeton City Council for three years when she was appointed to the legislature. In the Assembly, she is chair of the Higher Education Committee, vice-chair of the Tourism and Arts Committee and a member of the Transportation, Public Works and Independent Authorities Committee. Her most notable legislative achievement was sponsorship of a law that bans discrimination against the unemployed in job listings. Employers have often stated in their postings and ads that jobless applicants are not wanted. The law took effect on June 1, 2011, and was the first such ban in the United States.

ASSEMBLYMAN JOSEPH W. CHINNICI

Joseph W. Chinnici of Bridgeton represented the First Legislative District (Cape May County and part of Cumberland County) as an assemblyman from 1971 to 1987. He had been a city councilman for eight years, county freeholder for two years and freeholder director when he was elected to the Assembly. Chinnici was owner of Major Coat Co. of Bridgeton.

He became deputy speaker of the Assembly at the beginning of the 1986–87 session. But in 1987, he was indicted for bribing and giving kickbacks to an official of the Defense Personnel Supply Center in order to get military clothing contracts for his company. He maintained that he was involved in the case because he wanted to save his company and the jobs of his employees. He and the company pled guilty in 1988. U.S. district court judge Thomas N. O'Neill Jr. sentenced him to three years probation and three hundred hours of community service in June 1988. In pronouncing the lenient sentence, the judge said he had to consider the many letters he received in support of Chinnici and the man's exemplary public career. Judge O'Neill said that Chinnici had done an evil thing but the "actions were done by a good man who has spent his entire life in community service. He needs no rehabilitation."[78] Chinnici's case was part of a government investigation into corruption at the Defense Personnel Supply Center in Philadelphia. He died in 2007 at the age of eighty-seven.

STATE AND FEDERAL OFFICIALS

Three Bridgetonians became governors of New Jersey. They were Richard Howell (1792–1801), Joseph Bloomfield (1801–2, 1803–12) and Elias Seeley (February 1833–October 1833).

John Moore White was attorney general of New Jersey (1833–38). He was also a justice of the New Jersey Supreme Court (1838–45).

Several Bridgetonians also served as associate justices of the New Jersey Supreme Court. They were Daniel Elmer (1841–45), Lucius Q.C. Elmer (1852–59, 1861–69) and Thomas W. Trenchard (1906–41). Judge Trenchard presided over the Lindbergh kidnapping trial.

Bridgetonians served as legislators on state and federal levels. Dr. Jonathan Elmer was a United States senator (March 1789–March 1791). He was also a representative in Congress (1776, 1777, 1781, 1783, 1787 and 1789). General Ebenezer Elmer (1801–7), L.Q.C. Elmer (1843–45) and James G. Hampton (1845–49) all served in the U.S. Congress.

John T. Nixon served in the U.S. Congress (1859–63). Nixon was a judge of the U.S. District Court from 1870 until his death in 1889. He and General

Pauline Boykin, the first African American woman elected to Bridgeton City Council, was a much-respected and much-loved artist, teacher and public servant. She died in 1993. *Courtesy of the Boykin family.*

Ebenezer Elmer and L.Q.C. Elmer had served as members of the New Jersey legislature. General Elmer and John Nixon had been speakers of the New Jersey Assembly as well.

Jonathan Bowen, David Potter and Eli Elmer were members of the State Convention in Trenton that ratified the United States Constitution in 1787.

FIFTY YEARS OF FIRSTS

Since the middle of the twentieth century, Bridgeton's minority groups have been represented in city government. Albert B. Kelly has been the mayor since 2010 and is the first African American elected to that post. He had been a member of city council. He is president and

CEO of Gateway Community Action Partnership, a large anti-poverty organization. Gladys Lugardo-Hemple, who was elected at the same time, is the city's first Latina council member. Fanny S. Cowell was the first woman elected to Bridgeton City Council; she served as council president in 1967. Councilman Solomon Riley was the first African American elected to city office in Bridgeton's history in 1974. In 1978, Pauline Boykin became the first African American woman elected to city council. She was a member of city council for thirteen years and served on the board of education for six years.

CHAPTER 9

REVIVAL

Bridgeton's slide from prosperity to decay was gradual, and the climb back is gradual. A Master Plan completed in 1976 provided hope, encouragement and concrete proposals for a turnaround in the town's fortunes. The Master Plan gave an assessment of Bridgeton's amenities, especially the park, with its ball fields, playgrounds and zoo. The plan included the Cohansey River and the city's lakes in the list of assets. The document was straightforward about the liabilities:

> Like all older cities, Bridgeton is faced with urban problems and inadequate resources to solve these problems. It has older buildings, an incomplete street system and less than adequate public transport service…environmental pollution, etc.,…non-compatible land uses exist side by side…while the list of problems is long and seems exhaustive, none of these problems are insurmountable. The problems are not unique but common to cities throughout the nation.

When Mayor Donald H. Rainear and his running mates took office in 1978 (using the slogan "Bring Back Bridgeton"), they were well aware of the liabilities and anxious to promote Bridgeton's assets. The city's harsh decline was the greatest liability, and it proved to be a perverse asset.

In the 1960s and 1970s, many cities succumbed to the bulldozer method of urban renewal. Blocks of old, often architecturally valuable buildings were leveled to make way for new, often tasteless structures. Bridgeton possessed neither the money nor the will for many such "improvements." As a result, the city retained blocks of homes, stores and churches that had been built during its golden age. A 1979 survey by Hugh McCauley Associates of

Bridgeton Rose Vase by Acme Cut Glass Works of Bridgeton (1915–22). Note the two roses, one wild and one cultivated, on the vase. This product of the city's golden age is on exhibit at the Wheaton Museum of Glass Arts. *Photo by Flavia Alaya.*

Philadelphia, commissioned by the city government, revealed those buildings to be an unexpected asset and perhaps the key to Bridgeton's revival. The survey recommended tourism as a potential industry.

The city became the largest certified historic district in the state when it was placed on the National Register of Historic Places in 1982. The district includes 2,200 residential, commercial and church buildings of the Victorian, Colonial and Federal periods. The buildings are one-third of Bridgeton's architecture. They are not confined to one section of town but dot almost every neighborhood.

The city's high unemployment rate (at one point, over 14 percent) and depressed economy almost guaranteed aid through state and federal programs. The transformation and beautification began in 1980, when the cement sidewalks at the center of town were replaced with brick walks. Many Bridgetonians were skeptical. The town needed new industry, not new sidewalks. A sturdy and easy-to-maintain variety of locust tree (known as the Regents Scholar tree) was planted along the downtown sidewalks, and ersatz gaslights replaced the old lampposts. The downtown riverfront, another neglected resource, was rebuilt and beautified with greenery, fountains and benches. Development of the riverfront continued with construction of a marina and dredging of the waterway. Despite all the improvements, tourism did not take hold. The city's park, riverfront, historic district and cultural diversity did not reach their potential as attractions for visitors.

A NEW ZONING CODE

The most recent Master Plan for Bridgeton was completed in 2008. It proposed actions that could lead to improvement in the near future (five years). It listed eighty-five priorities that deal with housing problems, transportation failures and economic development needs. The plan's first priority was the revision of the zoning ordinance.

Since January 2011, a city council–sponsored committee has met biweekly to revise the outdated 1977 zoning ordinance, which has ninety-three sections written in bureaucratic language. After the revised code undergoes a stringent review by the planning board and a public hearing and is adopted by city council, it will become law.

An up-to-date zoning code would allow more flexibility in property use and simplify the zoning application process for building, changing or adding onto properties and structures. It will be a boon for builders, developers, landlords and homeowners. Through less restrictive regulations, it will eliminate the need for some variances, such as those presently required for second-floor living in the downtown area.

A DAMAGED PARK

The city park is one of the largest parks of its kind in the eastern United States. It continues as a mainstay of Bridgeton as a recreation center. Since January 2012, a committee has been at work to develop a long-range plan for the park. This group includes representatives from the Zoological Society and Historic Commission and members of city agencies, including the public works and recreation departments, city council, the city planner and the business administrator.

The flood of August 2011 has left the park in a sorry state, so planning for its future is an encouraging development. Fourteen inches of rain fell in mid-August after a prolonged dry spell. Two weeks later, Hurricane Irene swept through the area, but the damage was already done. The dam at Sunset Lake had already failed. The roadway along the lake sank, and the raceway (canal) through the park was also damaged. Sunset Lake is a dry bed now, and the raceway is reduced to a series of puddles. The storms toppled trees, limbs and brush throughout the park, and all the water emptied into the Cohansey River.

Agencies involved in repairing the damage and clearing the park are the Federal Emergency Management Agency (FEMA), the New Jersey

Department of Environmental Protection (DEP), the Bridgeton Public Works Department and numerous officials and agencies from the city, county, state and federal governments. The hurricane damaged a large section of the Northeast, so governmental response to that emergency took precedence over the August 14 storm, which affected a smaller area in Cumberland, Salem and Gloucester Counties in New Jersey. Official attention gradually focused on the local devastation, and several small projects are pending: removal of debris and trees along the raceway path, replacement of the brick walk at the Riverwalk senior complex and replacement of drainage pipes from the south end of the raceway to the head wall of the river behind the Nail Museum. Once the city engineer's plans have been approved by FEMA, the competitive bidding process can take place. Then the repair work can begin.[79]

CHANGING DEMOGRAPHICS

Social and economic changes have affected Bridgeton too. Bridgeton's population increased more than 10 percent between 2000 and 2010. It is larger than ever now at 25,349. The total for both census years includes about 3,000 inmates at the medium-security South Woods State Prison, which opened in 1997 on South Burlington Road. According to the 2010 census, Bridgeton residents include 8,274 whites, 8,996 African Americans and 153 Asians. The 11,046 Hispanics or Latinos form a group that makes up almost 44 percent of the population and takes in all racial classifications.[80] That population is made up of United States citizens, permanent residents and undocumented persons.

About 73 percent of the Hispanic/Latino residents are Mexicans, many from Oaxaca (pronounced *Wah-hawka*), the poorest state in Mexico. More than half the residents of Oaxaca live in extreme poverty. Many houses lack running water and indoor plumbing. Maternal and infant mortality rates are high because medical care is uncommon. Oaxacans have been leaving their birthplace for decades to escape the desperate conditions there. In recent years, male Oaxacans have come to the Bridgeton area to work in agriculture, landscaping or construction. The women perform domestic work, cleaning homes and offices. A small minority of Mexican immigrants, mostly women, speak only Zapotec, an indigenous language, rather than Spanish.

Bridgeton's downtown is growing with Mexican businesses of all types, including several restaurants. This population does strain Bridgeton's social services and healthcare systems,[81] but at the same time, it brings vitality

Above: On Cinco de Mayo, these young spectators join the crowds for the Mexican American celebration in downtown Bridgeton in May 2011. *Photo by Flavia Alaya.*

Left: Chief Mark Quiet Hawk Gould is the elected chief of the Nanticoke Lenni-Lenape tribe of Bridgeton, New Jersey, shown in 2012. *Photo by Cara Blume.*

to the community. The annual Cinco de Mayo celebration in downtown Bridgeton attracts some native Bridgetonians, as well as crowds of the Mexican newcomers.

About 350 Bridgetonians are of Native American descent, according to the 2010 census. But the data are unclear. It is not unlike the uncertainty about the numbers of Lenni-Lenape in the seventeenth century. In 1982, the Nanticoke Lenni-Lenape Indians of New Jersey, Inc., received official recognition as one of three New Jersey tribes. Tribal membership transcends state and municipal boundaries:

> *The tribe includes approximately three thousand enrolled tribal citizens, eighty percent of whom live in southern New Jersey and northern Delaware. Enrollment in the tribe requires documentation of blood relationship to core Nanticoke-Lenape families of southern New Jersey and the Delmarva Peninsula. The relationship is verified through birth certificates, death certificates, marriage certificates, tax records, census reports, and other documents. The Bridgeton-based tribal nation is the northernmost of three interrelated tribes of Nanticoke and Lenape people who remain around the Delaware Bay. They are part of an intertribal union governed by a council of the elected chiefs from each tribe.*[82]

Nanticoke Lenni-Lenape tribal law and tradition forbid the tribe's promotion or involvement in casino gaming or any business that profits from the promotion of vice. The definition of vice includes the sale of alcohol, tobacco and illegal substances. The tribe does not censure other tribes for their position on gaming but simply asserts its own "sovereign right."[83]

CONGREGATIONS IN TRANSITION

Bridgeton's only synagogue closed in 2008, its numbers reduced to about twenty families because members had died or moved away. Congregation Beth Abraham merged immediately with Temple Beth Hillel in Carmel to form Temple Beth Hillel Beth Abraham at the Carmel location. Congregation Beth Abraham sold the synagogue on Fayette Street to the City of Bridgeton. After extensive renovations, the city police department, municipal court and other city offices moved into the building in April 2009. The old city hall on East Commerce Street was built in 1931 with a small courtroom and other features suitable for its time but was inadequate for twenty-first-century needs. The building is now vacant. The Fayette Street building is handicapped-accessible and more suitable for public meetings, and the courtroom is more spacious than the old one.

Immaculate Conception and St. Teresa of Avila, the two Roman Catholic parishes in Bridgeton, merged with three smaller parishes in Rosenhayn, Cedarville and Port Norris to form the Parish of the Holy Cross in 2010. The main office of the new parish is at the St. Teresa site on Central Avenue. The church buildings remain open for worship at present. The merger was part of the restructuring of the Roman Catholic Diocese of Camden, brought about by a drastic decline in the number of priests. Bridgeton's Episcopal congregation has undergone changes as well. St. Andrew's Episcopal Church now shares a priest with Trinity Episcopal Church in Vineland. Immaculate Conception Regional School, which closed and then reopened as Our Lady of Guadalupe Regional School in 2007, closed permanently in 2009. That same year, the Bridgeton Board of Education began to lease the building for use as HOPE Academy, a small alternative high school.

CHANGING INDUSTRIES

The big three industries of Bridgeton's prosperous past are no longer major influences on the local economy. In 1966, Leone Industries, a manufacturer of glass containers, opened a plant on South East Avenue. The company is Bridgeton's only glass factory and employs 325 workers. It was recently sold to the Ardagh Group, a multinational company. All the sewing factories are gone. The Val Mode sewing factory on Broad Street has been transformed into Riverwalk Apartments for senior citizens. The Martin Corporation, a longtime textile company, remains the lone representative of that business in Bridgeton. The old-time food companies have left, replaced by White Wave, with 100 employees, and Buona Vita, with 55.

Seabrook Brothers and Sons thrives as a major business. Since 1978, the company has operated a plant that processes fresh vegetables in Upper Deerfield. The new Seabrook model rivals the old Seabrook Farms as an agribusiness. It employs just 450 workers, one-tenth the workforce of Seabrook Farms in the 1940s and 1950s. But through the use of twenty-first-century technology, it produces 150 million pounds of frozen vegetables a year, more than the old plant. Several great-grandsons of C.F. Seabrook are involved in the company, and the president is James M. Seabrook Jr., another great-grandson.

For the most part, Bridgeton's largest employers are involved in service or support industries. South Woods State Prison has a workforce of 1,000. The Bridgeton Board of Education employs 980 on its staff. South Jersey Healthcare employs 500 people in Bridgeton. Cumberland County employs 750 workers but not all of them in Bridgeton. Gateway Community Action Partnership, the anti-poverty agency, employs 398.

OBSTACLES

Bridgeton struggles to overcome some dire statistics. The official unemployment rate in 2012 is 12.8 percent. A high poverty rate (27.7 percent, compared with 9.1 percent for New Jersey) and lack of education hamper Bridgeton's economic growth. In New Jersey as a whole, 87.3 percent of residents over twenty-five are high school graduates. In Bridgeton, that number is 61.4 percent.[84] The crime rate is worrisome, too. It is much higher than the national and state averages. Crime rates for Millville and Vineland are higher than state and national rates as well, but overall crime declined in Cumberland County between 2005 and 2010. Violent crime in Bridgeton decreased 10.8 percent between 2006 and 2010. The number of robberies decreased from 156 in 2006 to 126 in 2010. Motor vehicle theft is much lower for Bridgeton than the state and national averages for that crime.[85] Mayor Albert B. Kelly proposed a fifteen-point crime prevention program for the city in 2011. His plan requires the involvement of the whole community: homes, schools, churches and even the offenders. His strategy includes an anti-littering campaign, a gun

Albert B. Kelly is the first African American mayor of Bridgeton, elected in 2010. He has also served on the Bridgeton Board of Education and city council. *Courtesy of Gateway Community Action Partnership.*

return program, a longed-for but not-assured increase in the number of police officers and an anonymous "tip line" to report crime.

INNOVATION

Bridgeton has inspired attention and concern beyond its borders. Rutgers University has invested its resources in Bridgeton, with a plan to spur growth through the town's traditional strength as an agricultural center. In 2001, the Rutgers Food Innovation Center opened in rented quarters on East Commerce Street. In 2008, the center built a new twenty-three-thousand-square-foot facility on East Broad Street. As its name implies, the center fosters innovation in all aspects of food-related businesses, from farms to food service companies. Growth and development of South Jersey agriculture through technology and an entrepreneurial spirit is a special goal

The Sheppard House, once known as Ivy Hall, built in 1791. The building is now occupied by the Cousteau Coastal Center of Rutgers University and has been a school for girls, a maternity hospital and a restaurant. *Photo by Sam Feinstein.*

of the center. Clients can use the facility's equipment to test their products for a reasonable fee and can consult the staff for business guidance too. The center has assisted over one thousand clients, who come from a wide area. Since he was an assemblyman, New Jersey Secretary of Agriculture Douglas H. Fisher has been a keen supporter of the Food Innovation Center.

The Cousteau Coastal Center of Rutgers University has occupied the 1791 David Sheppard House since 2008. The lovely Federal-style building was completely restored with help from a grant of the New Jersey Historic Trust and collaboration between the City of Bridgeton and Rutgers. The Cousteau Coastal Center is a marine sciences educational facility and an offshoot of the Rutgers Jacques Cousteau National Estuarine Research Reserve. The center offers activities and programs about marine science for schools, from kindergarten through twelfth grade, and professional training for teachers. Adult and professional seminars and activities for volunteers are also presented there. The programs make a connection between marine science and daily life in the area.

SUPPORT

Local nonprofit organizations also strive to support Bridgeton. For example, the Bridgeton High School Stadium Foundation raised $4.8 million to rebuild the stadium. The original purpose was renovation, but the old stadium could not be fixed. A group of interested citizens began to organize to raise funds for the project in 2006 through the encouragement of Victor Gilson, who was Bridgeton superintendent of schools at the time. The stadium was rebuilt and dedicated in April 2012 as the Jim Hursey Stadium at the Robert C. Thompson Family Sports Complex, keeping the name of the old stadium and adding the name of Thompson, who donated $1 million for the new facility. A combination of government and private funds made up the remainder. The foundation will continue to raise funds on behalf of the high school.

The Bridgeton city park benefits from the activity of the New Sweden Colonial Farmstead and Living History Center, another nonprofit. In 1987, the New Sweden Farmstead Museum was built in the city park to commemorate the 350th anniversary of the arrival of Swedish colonists in America. During festivities in 1988, King Carl XVI Gustaf and Queen Silvia of Sweden dedicated the replica of a farmstead village. The entire village of log cabins was built employing the authentic seventeenth-century methods of the Swedish colonists. Restoration of the structures is underway.

The Farmstead will be revived as a living history center in time to celebrate the 375th anniversary in 2013. Colonial craft and cooking demonstrations, school programs and other special events are planned for the year.

Bridgeton Main Street, founded in 1990, is a nonprofit organization that devotes its resources to the entire community. It is the oldest Main Street Association in the state, funded by Urban Enterprise Zone grants. Main Street's director and volunteers work in tandem with local government, civic groups and individuals for the economic revival and improvement of Bridgeton. Though the goal is serious, Main Street works toward it by means of enjoyable events that bring people together in Bridgeton's downtown. The Food-Film-Fest is an evening centered on an ethnic menu and movie. In 2012, the theme was Mexican food, cooked by local chefs, and the movie was *Like Water for Chocolate*. The Cinco de Mayo celebration in downtown Bridgeton, the Cohansey Riverfest and Crabfest and the outdoor market in the culinary district are other well-attended events. The purpose is to establish Bridgeton as a culinary destination, with a variety of restaurants. This dovetails with the aims of the Food Innovation Center.

Rutgers University and nonprofit groups like Main Street share a strategy of showcasing the town's assets to boost the economy. Working alone, no nonprofit group, service club, single business or even government, no matter how well intentioned, can restore Bridgeton's prosperity. But community goodwill and cumulative energy might accomplish it. Bridgeton developed and thrived because of the Cohansey River. An almost unnoticed section of the 2008 Master Plan states that there is "need to turn the city around and face the river."[86] Perhaps the key to regaining prosperity can be found there.

NOTES

CHAPTER 1

1. Anne S. Woodruff and F. Alan Palmer, *The Unalachtigo: The Original People of Cumberland County* (Cumberland County, NJ: Cumberland County Historical Society, 1973), 16.
2. Richard P. McCormick, *New Jersey from Colony to State: 1609–1789* (New Brunswick, NJ: Rutgers University Press, 1964), 38.
3. Recorded in Salem Book One, 176. It is an official book of records, surveys and deeds on file in Salem County.
4. Thomas Cushing, MD, and Charles E. Sheppard, Esq., *History of the Counties of Gloucester, Salem, and Cumberland, New Jersey* (Woodbury, NJ: Gloucester County Historical Society, reprinted 1974), 316.
5. John E. Pomfret, *Colonial New Jersey: A History* (New York: Charles Scribner's Sons, 1973), 38.
6. *New Jersey Records, Book B, Part II, Fenwick Surveys, 1676–1705.*
7. L.Q.C. Elmer, *History of the Early Settlement and Progress of Cumberland County, New Jersey* (Bridgeton, NJ: George F. Nixon, Publisher, 1869), 6.
8. Thanks to Cumberland County historian Jonathan Wood for this insight.
9. John E. Pomfret, *The New Jersey Proprietors and Their Lands, 1664–1776* (Princeton, NJ: D. Van Nostrand Co., Inc., 1964), 25.
10. McCormick, *New Jersey from Colony to State*, 46.
11. Elmer, *History of the Early Settlement*, 62.
12. Isaac T. Nichols, *The City of Bridgeton, New Jersey: Its Settlement and Growth, 1889* (Philadelphia: Burk & McFetridge, Printers, 1889), 11.

CHAPTER 2

13. The identity of the builder of the first Cohansey Bridge was unknown for many years. Rulon Brooks Sr., who was a resident of Clark's Pond in the twentieth century, revealed a deposition made in 1739 by his ancestor, Seth Brooks.

14. Until 1752, the first day of a new year was March 25. So if the reader looks at the dates with a modern calendar, the day was January 19, 1748. If the old calendar is followed, it was 1747.

15. Taken from the application for a tavern license.

16. Cushing and Sheppard, *History of the Counties*, 582–83.

17. Ibid., 583.

CHAPTER 3

18. Francis A. Stanger Jr., *Bridgeton: Gem-o'-Jersey* (Bridgeton, NJ: Calendar Ad Service, 1926), 8.

19. Cushing and Sheppard, *History of the Counties*, 541.

20. William C. Mulford, *Historical Tales of Cumberland County, New Jersey* (Bridgeton, NJ: Evening News Co., 1941), journal from May 2, 1775–December 14, 1775, 35.

21. Jonathan Elmer, "Address to the Inhabitants of Cumberland County," Personal Papers, Jonathan Elmer, Library of Congress.

22. Taken from an eighteenth-century petition to keep an inn.

23. Philip Vickers Fithian was a Presbyterian clergyman whose journals are regarded as valuable sources of eighteenth-century lore. He spent time in Virginia as a tutor, and his recollections are mandatory reading for tour guides in today's Williamsburg.

24. Cushing and Sheppard, *History of the Counties*, 617.

25. From the first public notice advertising the *Plain Dealer*.

26. Ibid.

27. Introduction to a reprint of the existing copies of the *Plain Dealer*, published by William Nelson, 1894. Nelson's publication relied on handwritten copies made by Thomas Harris in 1776,

28. Charles L. Scarani, *Ringing Through History: Cumberland County's Liberty Bell* (n.p., n.d.), ch. 4.

CHAPTER 4

29. Isaac Nichols, *City of Bridgeton, New Jersey*, 18.

30. Cushing and Sheppard, *History of the Counties*, 559.

31. From Brearley Lodge No. 9, "Memorandum of Agreement," February 21, 1797.

32. Elmer, *History of the Early Settlement*, 63.

33. Ibid.

34. Ibid.

35. Ibid. Harris incorrectly identified the disease as measles.

36. Mulford, *Historical Tales of Cumberland County*, 111.

37. George W. McCowan, *City of Bridgeton, N.J., 1881* (Bridgeton, NJ: McCowan and Nichols, 1881), 4–5.

38. Cushing and Sheppard, *History of the Counties*, 551.

CHAPTER 5

39. Description based on William C. Mulford's account of Bridgeton in 1850, *The Town of Bridgeton, N.J., 1850, The Past Compared with the Present* (Bridgeton, NJ, 1937).

40. Isaac T. Nichols, *Historic Days in Cumberland County, New Jersey, 1855–1865* (Bridgeton, NJ: Isaac Nichols, publisher, 1907), 36.

41. Nichols, *City of Bridgeton, New Jersey*, 20.

42. Nichols, *Historic Days*, 62.

43. Nichols, *City of Bridgeton, New Jersey*, 19.

44. Hugh J. McCauley Associates, *Historic Site Survey, Bridgeton, New Jersey*, part III (Philadelphia, 1979), 13.

45. Nichols, *City of Bridgeton, New Jersey*, 28.

46. For a more detailed account of Smith's life and character, see Arthur J. Cox and Thomas Malim, *Ferracute: The History of an American Enterprise* (Bridgeton, NJ: A.J. Cox, publisher, 1985).

47. William B. Kirby, *Art Issue of the Bridgeton Evening News—A Souvenir of Bridgeton, N.J.* (Bridgeton, NJ: J. Ward Richardson, 1895), 91.

48. *Boyd's Cumberland County Directory, 1881–1882* (Philadelphia: C.E. Howe Co., 1881).

49. *Boyd's Cumberland County Directory, 1891–1892* (Philadelphia: C.E. Howe Co., 1891).

50. Cushing and Sheppard, *History of the Counties*, 590.

51. Bridgeton High School junior and senior classes, *City of Bridgeton, New Jersey*, compilations of articles by students, 1921, 17.

52. Kirby, *Art Issue*, 62.

53. Margaret Louise Mints, *Lighthouse to Leeward* (Port Norris, NJ: Margaret L. Mints, publisher, 1976), 68–69.

54. Kirby, *Art Issue*, 77.

CHAPTER 6

55. *Bridgeton Evening News*, November 23, 1927, 1.

56. Stanger, *Bridgeton: Gem-o'-Jersey*, 18.

57. George Agnew Chamberlain, *The Lantern on the Plow* (New York: Harper and Bros., 1924), 290–91.

58. *Dollar Weekly News* (Bridgeton, NJ), August 10, 1934, 2.

59. Shirley R. Bailey and Jim Parkhurst, *Early South Jersey Amusement Parks* (Millville, NJ: South Jersey Publishing Co., 1977, repr. 1990), 5.

60. Betty Zane, *…And That Was Entertainment Back in Bridgeton's Good Old Days* (Bridgeton, NJ: Bridgeton High School student government, 1976), 10–13.

61. Statistics on the 1920s from Stanger, *Bridgeton: Gem-o'-Jersey*, 11–15.

62. *We Women*, October 1952, 22.

63. From *Dollar Weekly News* accounts (Bridgeton, NJ), April and August 1924.

64. See William A.M. Steward and Rev. Theophilus G. Steward, DD, *Gouldtown, A Very Remarkable Settlement of Ancient Date* (Philadelphia: Lippincott Co., 1913), for complete story of Gouldtown's original families.

65. Congregation Beth Abraham, *Commemorating Dedication of the New Sanctuary* (Bridgeton, NJ: Congregation Beth Abraham, 1971).

66. Sharron Morita, "Life Goes On," *Bridgeton Journal*, May 21, 1992, 1, 4.

67. John M. Seabrook, *The Henry Ford of Agriculture: Charles F. Seabrook 1881–1964 and Seabrook Farms 1893–1959* (Seabrook, NJ: Seabrook Educational and Cultural Center, 1995). This memoir was written by C.F.'s youngest son, Jack.

68. Charles H. Harrison, *Growing a Global Village: Making History at Seabrook Farms* (New York: Holmes and Meier, 2003), 42.

69. Statistics from *Seabrook: Henry Ford of Agriculture*, 51.

70. Harrison, *Growing a Global Village*, 29.

71. Lloyd S. Kelling, *Historical Study of a Strike at Seabrook Farms, Inc., 1934* (Glassboro, NJ: Glassboro State College, 1969), 50–51.

72. *Seabrook: Henry Ford of Agriculture*, 26.

73. American Friends Service Committee, Philadelphia and Baltimore, *A Year in the Life… Bridgeton High School, Bridgeton, New Jersey, 1971* (Philadelphia: Committee, publisher, 1972), 91–92.

CHAPTER 7

74. Roger E. Nathan, *The Saga of South Jersey Healthcare: From Country Medicine to County Mergers to Regional Giant, A Story of Pride and Progress* (Bridgeton, NJ: South Jersey Healthcare Museum Committee, 2004), 8.

75. Ibid., 154.

76. John George, "Objections Overcome in Hospital Deal: Construction Begins on the First New Hospital in South Jersey in Decades; a $91M Project," *Philadelphia Business Journal*, December 14, 2001. www.accessmylibrary.com/article-1G1-81229143/objections-overcome-hospital-deal.html.

77. Penelope S. Watson, *Banknotes and Books for Bridgeton: A History of 150 East Commerce Street* (Bridgeton, NJ: Save the Library!, 2011), 24.

CHAPTER 8

78. *Bridgeton Evening News*, June 1, 1988, 1.

CHAPTER 9

79. Thanks to Dean Dellaquila, director of the Bridgeton Public Works Department, for this information.
80. The total of these numbers does not equal 25,349. In the tabulations, racial categories overlap and include biracial and multiracial individuals.
81. Sarah Birdsall, Planning Consulting, *A Community Vision for the City of Bridgeton*, February 2010, 4.
82. Thanks to Pastor John Norwood, who is a member of the Nanticoke Lenni-Lenape Tribal Nation, for this clarification.
83. John R. Norwood, *We Are Still Here! The Tribal Saga of New Jersey's Nanticoke and Lenape Indians*, (Moorestown: Native New Jersey Publications, 2007), 32.
84. These statistics are from United States Census Bureau Quickfacts.
85. These statistics are from the FBI's Uniform Crime Reports database.
86. Environmental Resolutions, Inc., Mount Laurel, New Jersey, 08054, *Master Plan: City of Bridgeton, New Jersey*, September 2008, III-2.

INDEX

ABOUT THE AUTHOR

Tales of rumrunners and speakeasies; arrowheads and pottery shards; Oberlin Smith, Charlie Seabrook and Sylvia Beach; circuit-riding priests; Quaker social activism; Klansmen wearing telltale shoes; and a napping editor all fueled Sharron Morita's fascination with Bridgeton history. She began to hear such stories when she arrived in Bridgeton to work as a reporter and editor after graduation from Syracuse University with a degree in journalism and political science. Later work as a freelance writer added to her supply of tales about the town.

She contributed to *New Jersey: Spotlight on Government*, a publication of the New Jersey League of Women Voters, and wrote *Bridgeton Impressions: 1686–1986* for Bridgeton's 300th anniversary celebration. In 1995, she received the Lloyd P. Burns Memorial Award for responsible journalism from the New Jersey Press Association.